THE INDEPENDENT LOCOMOTIVE BUILDERS

THE INDEPENDENT LOCOMOTIVE BUILDERS

An Overall Historical Survey

Anthony Burton

PEN & SWORD
TRANSPORT
AN IMPRINT OF PEN & SWORD BOOKS LTD.
YORKSHIRE – PHILADELPHIA

First published in Great Britain in 2025 by
Pen and Sword Transport
An imprint of
Pen & Sword Books Ltd.
Yorkshire – Philadelphia

ISBN 978 1 03611 413 8

A CIP catalogue record for this book is available from the British Library.

Typeset in 11.5/15.5 pt Palatino by SJmagic DESIGN SERVICES, India.

Printed and bound in India by Replika Press Pvt. Ltd.

The Publisher's authorised representative in the EU for product safety is Authorised Rep Compliance Ltd., Ground Floor, 71 Lower Baggot Street, Dublin D02 P593, Ireland.
www.arccompliance.com

For a complete list of Pen & Sword titles please contact

PEN & SWORD BOOKS LIMITED
George House, Beevor Street, Off Pontefract Road, Hoyle Mill, Barnsley, South Yorkshire, England, S71 1HN.
E-mail: enquiries@pen-and-sword.co.uk
Website: www.pen-and-sword.co.uk

or

PEN AND SWORD BOOKS
1950 Lawrence Rd, Havertown, PA 19083, USA
E-mail: uspen-and-sword@casematepublishers.com
Website: www.penandswordbooks.com

MIX
Paper | Supporting responsible forestry
FSC™ C016779
www.fsc.org

Contents

Introduction

When one thinks of locomotive manufacturers, the first thoughts probably turn to the works of the great railway companies, such as Swindon and Crewe. They were certainly hugely important, and many railway companies did build for their own lines. There were also several industrial concerns, such as collieries that built a few locomotives for their own use. Throughout railway history there have been very many independents who sometimes built for the major companies when they needed more stock than they could supply for themselves. But they were also extremely important in supplying locomotives to a wide range of different customers and in building specialist locomotives, such as narrow gauge locomotives and the enclosed engines for street tramways. For many of these companies, however, the overseas market was even more important than the home, sending engines out to every continent. Many were innovators and several were noted for the very high quality of their craftsmanship. These are the independent builders we shall be looking at in this book. Some of the smaller suppliers will be listed with brief notes in the final chapter.

Chapter One

The Pioneers

In the years between the early experiments in developing locomotives to run on railed tracks and the opening of the Stockton & Darlington Railway (S&DR) in 1825, there were numerous engineers developing their own ideas on how they should be built. The early problem of heavy engines breaking brittle cast iron rails that had plagued Richard Trevithick was initially solved using a rack and pinion system that gave greater traction to a light engine. It was used on the world's first commercially successful railway that linked the Middleton Colliery near Leeds to the Aire & Calder Navigation and opened in June 1812. The system was devised by John Blenkinsop and the locomotive was built by Matthew Murray of Fenton, Murray & Wood in Leeds. Among those who came to see it was George Stephenson, who was to go on to build his first locomotive *Blücher* for the Killingworth Colliery, using many of the features that he had seen on the Middleton engine. The Winstanley colliery ordered a locomotive based on the Blenkinsop design from the Haig Foundry in nearby Wigan. It was delivered in 1812 and was followed by two more engines for the line. Other engineers also developed their own colliery engines, notably William Hedley at the Wylam Colliery. Construction would have relied heavily on the work of the Wylam foreman blacksmith, Timothy Hackworth. Quite what part Hackworth played in developing their first engine is now impossible to gauge, but he was to move on to become a major figure in locomotive development and one of the first of the independent manufacturers.

The S&DR owes it special place in railway history as being the first public railway to be authorised to use steam locomotives.

The Middleton colliery rack railway; the world's first successful commercial railway.

The chief engineer responsible for planning and constructing the line was Geroge Stephenson. He then had to consider who would build the locomotives. He approached Fenton, Murray and Wood but their reply was terse: 'It does not suit with the present arrangement of our Business to take orders for High Pressure and Locomotive Engines.' In fact, the company were to resume locomotive building in 1831, and we shall be taking a closer look at that in Chapter 4.

The alternative was for Stephenson, who had already designed an engine for Killingworth Colliery, to build for the line. A business was set up with Stephenson, Edward Pease, a manufacturer and principal promoter of the railway and Michael Longridge of the Bedlington Ironworks, a company that manufactured the wrought iron rails that were now replacing the older cast iron track. Eyebrows might have been raised if George Stephenson, chief engineer of the line, was seen to be ordering locomotives from George Stephenson, engine builder. So, the company was set up in the name of his 19-year-old son as Robert Stephenson & Co. The initial capital was £4,000 divided into ten equal shares. Pease held four shares; Longbridge and the two Stephensons two each – though Pease had to lend Robert the £400 for his share. Premises were acquired at Forth Street in Newcastle-upon-Tyne and the world's first specialist locomotive works opened for business.

There were new machine tools available. John Wilkinson had solved one problem for engine builders with his machine for accurately boring cylinders that had been used for the original Boulton & Watt engines. Matthew Murray had developed a planing machine that produced flat surfaces, which he used to construct the slide valves for the Middleton engine. This was considered so valuable an invention that to ensure it was kept secret, it was kept in a separate, locked room to which only certain workers were allowed access. Other planing machines were produced at the time. James Fox built a planer which ran on rollers and ran so true that it was said that if a sheet of paper was put under one of the rollers, the whole machine would stop. Richard Roberts built a planer in 1817 that is now in the Science Museum in London, and he was later to enter the world of locomotive manufacturing, with the formation of the company Sharp, Roberts & Co. So, Forth Street had the latest technology needed to make locomotives, but the first two engines to be built there for the S&DR, *Locomotion* and *Hope,* showed little if any improvement over the earlier Killingworth engine. Each had a single flue: the fire was lit at one end of the tube, contained by a firebrick wall, and the end of the flue poked out of the far end of the boiler and was turned up to form the chimney. The two cylinders were mounted vertically on the boiler and transferred the power via cross-heads and connecting links to crank pins on the wheels. There was no reversing gear, so the driver had to make the change manually, by assessing when steam had to be admitted to the cylinders, unclipping the connecting rods and reconnecting them when the appropriate position of the crank was obtained.

At first, however, they were only needed for the main work of the line, which was hauling coal, and passengers were carried in a conventional horse-drawn stage coach, fitted with flanged wheels so that it could be used on the track. The name Stockton & Darlington is a little misleading, as the end of the line was not at Darlington, but well beyond it at collieries north of the town. Workshops were set up at Shildon, a few miles north of Darlington, to maintain and build locomotives. The premises were fairly basic and set at the end of a short spur from the main line. The man in charge was Timothy Hackworth and he was soon to be kept busy.

Two other engines were added to the line but were of the same general design as the original and all gave trouble. The ride was rough – Stephenson experimented with 'steam springs' but they proved unsatisfactory. Raising enough steam proved problematic. Hackworth introduced a device first tried by Richard Trevithick, the blast pipe. Exhaust steam, instead of simply escaping out into the air, was passed to the bottom of the chimney, which had the effect of pulling air through the boiler, increasing the efficiency of the fire in the firebox. This was to become an essential part of later locomotives but is only effective if the extra heat can be used effectively. On these early engines, the effect was simply too fierce, and often resulted in burning coals being hurled out to start trackside fires.

There were reports of locomotives regularly running out of steam and the crew having to stop and wait for pressure to build before continuing with the journey. There were further problems with fractures to wheels. The engines were quite simply not living up to expectations, which is perhaps not too surprising for no engines had ever had to haul heavy loads over such a distance before. There was talk of abandoning locomotives altogether and returning to the use of horses. Something had to be done.

In the midst of all this activity, Robert Stephenson was offered the chance to travel to Colombia, to look at the possibility of developing silver mines in the interior and linking them by either rail or road to a port on the coast. There has been some speculation on why he accepted, having only recently been placed, nominally at least, in charge at Forth Street. It has been suggested that there was a disagreement between father and son, but alternative scenarios are possible. George may not actually have had a formal connection with the works, but it was his ideas and plans that prevailed there, and Robert might have been looking for a role that would give him full responsibility for a project. And there is one very obvious factor; it would be a rather dull young man who, offered the chance to visit somewhere as remote and exotic as South America was then, decided he would rather stay in Newcastle. Michael Longridge was to take over for what was expected to be a short time, but Robert left England in 1824 and did not return until 1827. His absence did nothing to help develop the Forth works as Longbridge struggled to cope with trying to manage, while still looking after his own affairs.

A new engine was delivered in 1827, designed at Forth Street by Robert Wilson. It was a four-cylinder engine, with each pair of wheels worked by cranks set at right angles to each other. It was not a success, but Hackworth received permission to use the boiler as the basis for a new locomotive for the line and a party of German engineers visited Shildon that year and recorded details of their talk with Hackworth and his various ideas for both four- and six-wheeled engines. Work began in 1827 on what would become the *Royal George*. It was very different in several respects from the earlier locomotives used on the line. It had six coupled wheels, a return-flue boiler, in which the firebox was at the same end of the engine as the chimney and the flue then bent round in a U-shape. The pistons were vertical and drove directly down to the trailing wheels. There were no facilities for turning large wheels at Shildon, so the centre hub was machined true, and the outer rim centred by means of wooden and iron plugs and wedges, a type that came to be known as 'plug wheels'. It was also fitted with a spring safety valve, designed by Hackworth. The new engine made its first run in November 1827 and continued in service until the end of 1840 and was then sold on to the Wingate Colliery, who paid more than it cost to build. It was a triumph for Hackworth, and the company rewarded him with a £20 bonus, which would have a purchasing power today of around £2,500 – a true mark of appreciation.

In 1829 a major challenge was thrown out to the world of engineering by the Liverpool & Manchester Railway (L&MR). There had been discussions on how the line should be run, some favouring a system of stationary engines, between which trains would be hauled by cable, the other arguing for locomotives. Experts were consulted, but failed to agree, so it was decided to hold a trial to see if anyone could build an engine suitable for hauling passengers and freight between the two cities. It was to take place at Rainhill in October 1829. The conditions laid down that the successful competitor had to complete the equivalent of a return journey along the whole route at an average speed of 10mph with a boiler pressure not more than 50 pounds per square inch (psi). There was also a restriction on weight – six tons maximum for a six-wheeled engine; four and a half tons for a four-wheel.

Robert Stephenson was now back at Forth Street and he at once began working on the design for what was then simply known as the 'premium engine'. The most revolutionary feature was the boiler and separate firebox. The idea had been suggested by the L&MR company secretary Henry Booth.

Instead of a single or return flue, it would have multiple small tubes carrying the hot gases through the boiler, greatly increasing the heating area. To make maximum use of the new system, blast pipe exhaust was used, which was now, finally, to prove invaluable. Another novel feature was the placing of the cylinders, which were no longer vertical but set at an angle of 45 degrees. Before being sent to Rainhill, the engine was given a name – *Rocket*.

Hackworth had continued developing his ideas for locomotives based on the *Royal George* with continued success, so it was inevitable that when the competition for the L&MR was announced he would have seen himself as having a very good chance of carrying away the prize. He faced, however, major problems. He had no financial backers, lacked the full range of facilities needed to build a locomotive and as a result had to rely on others to build different parts. The boiler was made at the Bedlington ironworks, the cylinders cast in Newcastle and other parts came from other manufacturers. Once all were gathered together, it was up to Hackworth to assemble them to make the engine which was, in effect, a scaled down version of *Royal George*, but carried on just four wheels. There was no time for much in the way of testing before the engine had to be taken to Rainhill.

Hackworth's engine which now had the name *Sans Pareil* got off to a bad start – it was overweight. It was, however, allowed to take part though no one was saying what would happen if it won. In the event, the engine was plagued with mechanical problems. At first it had been doing well, coasting along at a respectable 14mph, comfortably meeting the target speed. But then the boiler started leaking and the mechanics were up all night making repairs. The next run was on the 13th, which certainly proved unlucky for Hackworth. The boiler feed pump stopped working, no water was coming through, the firebox overheated, and the fusible plug that was there as a safety measure did what it was supposed to do, melted, allowing water to dowse the fire. Hackworth asked for time for more repairs, but the judges refused and *Sans Pareil*'s competition was over. The third competitor was *Novelty*, designed by Braithwaite and Ericsson, which we shall look at in more detail a little later.

To celebrate the 125th anniversary of the Rainhill Trials, replicas of the three main contestants were built. The replica *Sans Pareil* was constructed at what was then the British Rail workshops at Shildon, not far from where the original was assembled. I was present when the engine was rolled out of the shed, steamed and set off on its first journey. It was certainly an imposing sight and, but for the accidents, the original could almost certainly have met the speed requirements. It was actually purchased by the L&MR but was sold in 1831 to the Bolton & Leigh where it remained in service, after a few modifications, until 1844. By then, larger and far more powerful engines were in service, so it was sold again, this time to a colliery near Chorley and worked there right up to 1863. It was a sturdy workhorse, but represented the end of a period of construction, rather than the start of a new age. Nevertheless, Hackworth's reputation remained high.

The winner was, of course, *Rocket*, which was just as well as it was the engine that contained the features essential for further development. It was a major turning point in the history of Robert Stephenson & Co. and we shall be looking at their subsequent history in the next chapter. In the meantime, we'll see what happened to the other competitors.

In the years following the Rainhill Trials, Hackworth continued working for the S&DR, but he began to gain a new independence, taking personal control of Shildon and with the freedom to take on work in his own right and use all the facilities. In exchange, he was still required to keep the S&DR rolling stock running and was to pay 5 per cent per annum of the value of the property. By 1833, he gained complete independence and began building his own workshops at

Shildon including a foundry and erection shop. His new business card announced him as 'manufacturer of locomotive, marine, high pressure and other steam engines'. He was a true, independent locomotive builder.

Hackworth built several engines over the next few years and was among the first to supply locomotives for overseas railways. His first commission came from Russia. Nicholas I had come to power in 1825, but before that he had visited Britain and been impressed by the Middleton Colliery Railway. He supported the idea of a line that would join St. Petersburg to the Summer Palace at Tsarskoye Selo. It was very different from the locomotives he was building for colliery lines as the engine was to be used for passenger services. This was a 2-2-2 locomotive with 5ft diameter driving wheels and 3ft 6in leading and trailing wheels. Instead of a return flue boiler, this had a multi-tubular boiler, fitted with 135 1½ in tubes. The internal cylinders were 17in diameter but with just a 9in stroke, working a cranked axle. The gauge was measured in the Russian units of arshims and vershaks, which translated

The locomotive built by Timothy Hackworth for Russia's first railway.

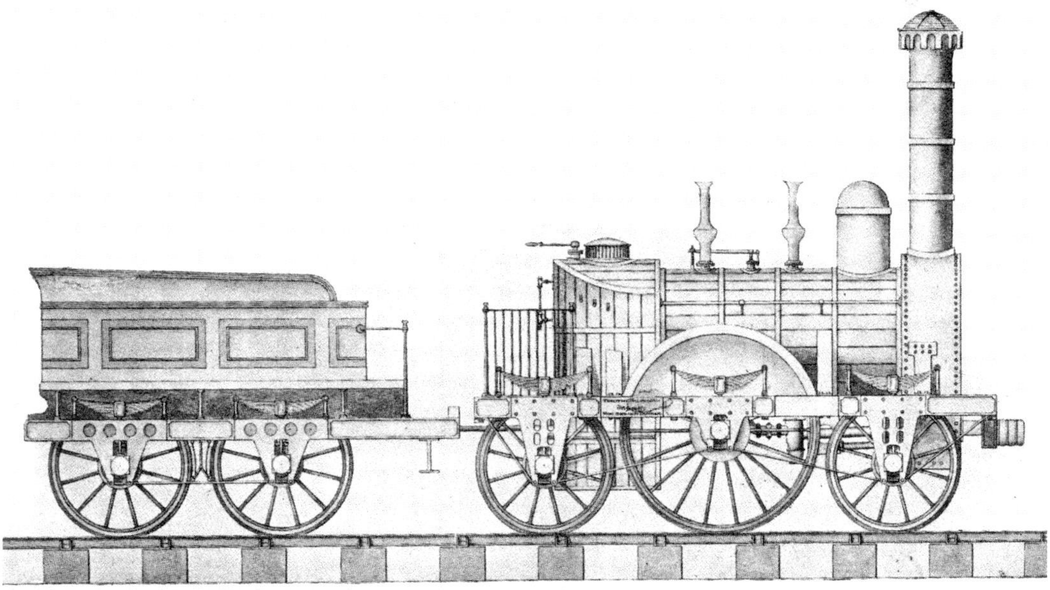

into 5ft 5in. Book keeping was obviously meticulous at Shildon, as the overall cost was given as £1,884 2s 9¾d.

The task of taking the engine to Russia fell to Timothy's 17-year-old son John and a Shildon foreman George Thomson. By the time they landed at a Baltic port, winter had set in and they continued the journey by sleigh – at one time being followed by a pack of wolves. For the young Hackworth it was an exotic experience and he left an account of the official blessing of the locomotive by Orthodox priests:

> Water was obtained from a neighbouring bog or 'stele' in a golden censer, and sanctified by immersions of a golden cross amid the chanting of choristers and intonations of priests while a hundred lighted tapers were held round it. This was followed by invocations of special blessings on the Tsar and Imperial Family, and fervent supplications that on all occasions of travel by the new mode, just being inaugurated, they might be well and safely conveyed. Then came the due Administration of the Ordinance by one priest bearing the holy censer, while a second, operating with a huge brush and dipping in the censer, dashed each wheel with the sign of the cross, with final copious showers all over the engine, of which John Hackworth was an involuntary partaker.

In spite of the elaborate blessing, there was an early problem when one of the cylinders cracked. Thomson had to set off on a 600-mile journey to the ordnance factory at Moscow, talking with him the details for casting a new cylinder, which was machined and then taken back to the engine, and travel resumed.

The other important overseas commission was for engines for Canada. The story begins in 1817 when Peter Crerar, a schoolteacher in Nova Scotia, sent plans to England for a railway linking the Albion collieries in Pictou County to the East River. He hoped to get expert advice and suggested that perhaps a British engineer might come to Canada to supervise the work.

***Samson*, built** by Hackworth for Canada's first railway.

But when the reply came it was full of praise for the work he had already done and suggested that he seemed perfectly capable of overseeing the work himself. He did and the result was a well-constructed line with no extravagant curves and no gradient steeper than 1:360 and was built to the British gauge of 4ft 8½in. It was originally worked by horses, but in 1838 it was decided to order locomotives and Timothy Hackworth was chosen to supply three engines – *Samson, John Buddle* and *Hercules. Samson* was the first to be delivered. All three were similar in many ways to *Royal George*, with six pug wheels, vertical cylinders above the rear wheels and a return flue boiler. *Samson* was a sturdy engine that did good work. The manager of the mines kept a record of work done by the engine between 1840 and 1853, where it was reported as averaging nearly 5,000 miles a year and hauling over 20,000 chauldrons of coal. The engine is now preserved at the Nova Scotia Museum of Industry.

Hackworth was to manufacture many engines, most of which were colliery engines that scarcely changed over the years. He was, however, also quite prepared to build locomotives designed by other engineers. He was approached by John Gray who had been one of the first to try to improve valve gear. In the early locomotives, there was always a fixed cut-off point when steam was admitted into the cylinder. His gear, known as the 'horse leg' allowed the cut-off point to be varied, but it was a complex system that was difficult to work, requiring a double action lever for the driver to operate. His first valve gear was fitted to a locomotive on the L&MR and he used it again on locomotives for the Hull & Selby Railway (H&SR), when he was appointed locomotive superintendent. In 1845 he was appointed to the same post on a far more important line, the London, Brighton & South Coast Railway. It was then that he put in an order with Hackworth for a series of twelve express locomotives, with single drive wheels.

The work was endlessly delayed through no fault of the Shildon works. Timothy and his son John were regular visitors to London, trying to sort out problems with the design. John, who seems to have been a good deal less tolerant than his father, became increasingly irritated. He wrote to Gray complaining that they were not receiving original plans but were forbidden from using any of their own. When plans did arrive, they were not always accurate – one, for a crank axle, for example, was so faulty that the axle would have been impossible to use. There were so many mistakes, he wrote, that he wished they had never taken on the work at all. The engines were, however, built – two completed in 1846, seven in 1847 and the last three the following year. Hackworth was not the only one exasperated by Gray – the company dismissed him. The engines themselves were a success and continued in use, with modifications, for nearly thirty years. The company acknowledged Hackworth's contribution in the 1890s by naming one of their express locomotives after him.

One of Hackworth's last engines was built in 1849 and as it incorporated all his ideas, he named it after his first engine – it too was *Sans Pareil.* The engine was a 2-2-2 passenger engine with inside cylinders and a crank axle, with a longitudinally welded boiler. On trials it hauled a train of six coaches over a distance of 45 miles in an hour and three minutes. The Hackworths were so impressed that John wrote to Robert Stephenson reminding him that their fathers had competed at Rainhill and challenging him to a new contest to match his best engine against the new *Sans Pareil.* The challenge was never taken up. It was to mark the end of Timothy Hackworth's career as he died the following year. John Hackworth took over the business, but soon moved to new works in Darlington, where he concentrated on stationary engines. There were to be no more Hackworth engines, but as one of the first independent manufacturers of locomotives, Timothy Hackwork had played a major role in railway history.

The other main competitors at Rainhill were John Braithwaite and John Ericsson, whose engine *Novelty* was based on an earlier design for a fire engine. It was a lightweight affair with a vertical boiler, which was destined like *Sans Pareil* to be unable to finish the competition. It was eventually to find a home working on the St. Helens & Runcorn Gap Railway. Braithwaite and Ericsson built two more locomotives, *William IV* and *Queen Adelaide* of a similar type, and after being tried on the Liverpool & Manchester, the company refused to buy them. Gorge Stephenson on seeing *Novelty* for the first time, remarked tersely 'no guts', which proved all too accurate. Ericsson went to America and enjoyed a successful career, while Braithwaite formed a new partnership, Braithwaite, Milner & Co., to build locomotives. Their biggest order came from America, when the Philadelphia & Reading Railroad ordered eight 0-4-0 locomotives, one of which, another *Rocket*, is preserved at Railroad Museum of Pennsylvania.

Rocket – not the famous Stephenson locomotive but one built by Braithwaite, Milner & Co. for the Reading & Pennsylvania Railroad. It is preserved at the Franklin Institute, Philadelphia.

Before leaving the Rainhill story, there is one other person who needs to be mentioned. John Urpeth Rastrick was one of the two engineers invited to report on which would be the more appropriate system for the L&MR – stationary engines or locomotives. They came to the ambiguous conclusion that although locomotives would be cheaper to buy than a set of stationary engines, the running costs would be higher – hence the Rainhill trials. He was a partner with James Foster in the company Foster, Rastrick. The company was based at Stourbridge and they built a number of locomotives for a local colliery, the last of which, *Agenoria* was completed in 1829 and is now preserved in the National Collection at York. They would hardly be noticed in railway history had they not received a visitor from America.

The visitor was Horatio Allen, who had been sent by the Delaware & Hudson Canal to purchase locomotives, preferably from Robert Stephenson & Co. The canal had been built to provide coal for New York, but it required a short section of railroad to join the colliery to the canal. Allen seems to have been impressed by the Stourbridge engine and although he ordered one engine from Stephenson, he ordered three from Foster, Rastrick, the first to be completed being the *Stourbridge Lion*. It was very similar to *Agenoria* with two vertical cylinders at the firebox end, with drive transmitted through a 'grasshopper' arrangement. The piston rods were attached to beams that were pivoted near one end, with the connecting rods to the wheels attached to the other. The fire grate was divided in two to feed two separate riveted tubes that ended an unusually tall chimney, with its top 22ft above the rails. Although a Stephenson locomotive was the first to reach America, it was the *Stourbridge Lion* that was the first to be run, with Allen himself on the footplate. 'I took my position on the platform of the locomotive alone, and with my hand on the throttle-valve said: "If there is any danger in this ride, it is not necessary that more than one be subjected

***Agenoria* built** by Foster, Rastrick & Co. for the Kingswinsford Railway, now in the National Railway Museum, York.

to it".' He declared himself well satisfied with the result, but the spectators who had come to watch the great event, were horrified to see the wooden trestle bridge sway alarmingly as the engine passed over it. The track had been laid with strap rails, wooden with just an iron strip on top, which proved wholly inadequate to take the weight of the locomotive. The first locomotive to run on a commercial railway in America was wheeled away to a shed and never ran again.

One other of the early pioneers, who had been associated with the Stephensons as a director of Robert Stephenson & Co, Michael Longridge, began manufacturing locomotives at his R.B. Longridge works at Bedlington in Northumberland in 1838. The year before, he had constructed a locomotive for the Stanhope & Tyne Railway, presumably at the nearby Bedlington Iron Works. Between 1838 and 1840, he built a number of 2-2-2s for European companies, including *De Arend,* the first locomotive to go into service in the

A replica of the *Stourbridge Lion* built by Foster, Rastrick – the first locomotive to run in America. It was constructed for the US National Museum.

Netherlands. A replica, built for the centenary, is now in the Netherlands Railway Museum. He also supplied two 0-4-2s for the German states. A distinguishing feature of the engines was the tall, ornate dome immediately behind the chimney. There was a gap in production, which restarted in 1843, with just two locomotives being built, but things improved considerably in 1846, and there were orders from many different companies for mainly six-wheeled locomotives, including broad gauge engines for the Bristol & Exeter Railway. A more unusual broad gauge was built for the South Devon, a domeless 4-4-0 saddle tank. The last locomotive to be built was an 0-4-0 well tank for the Holyhead Breakwater constructors in 1852.

Chapter Two

Robert Stephenson & Co.

The years after the Rainhill trials saw huge advances being made by the company. *Rocket* had been constructed to meet the very specific conditions laid down for the competition. Now, with those restrictions removed, changes could be made. Four locomotives, *Meteor, Comet, Dart* and *Arrow* were basically similar to Rocket, apart from the cylinders which had now been lowered from an angle of 45° to an almost horizontal position – *Rocket*'s cylinders would also be lowered in time. The next two engines to be built at Forth Street, *Phoenix* and *North Star*, contained an innovation, a smoke box at the foot of the chimney. This served a dual purpose; it increased the effect of the exhaust blast and made access to the tubes for cleaning and maintenance far easier. These engines were also bigger in every sense, with cylinder bore increasing from the 8in of *Rocket* to 11in, the number of boiler tubes going up from 25 to 130 and the engines themselves were heavier. The last of the group weighed 8 tons against the 4½ tons of *Rocket*. One passenger who travelled on the line before the official opening was Thomas Creevey, who took the trouble to time a part of his journey, using his pocket watch, which had a second hand, so seems to have provided an accurate idea of the speed of these early engines in service. Over a distance of five miles, the average speed was 20mph, but at one point reached 23mph. This seems quite leisurely to us, but to Creevey it was '*frightful*, really flying, and it is impossible to divest yourself of the notion of instant death to all upon the least accident happening'. There was also a suggestion that the blast-pipe exhaust was proving too efficient, as several ladies in the party had holes burned in their clothes from flying embers from the chimney.

All these engines were intended for use on the L&MR, but there was also an engine built for the Canterbury & Whitstable, an odd little line partly worked by locomotive and partly worked by cable haulage up an incline. The engine *Invicta* was very similar to *Rocket*, except that the cylinders were set at the chimney end of the boiler. It was not a great success, but in May 1830 it had the distinction of operating the first passenger service to be worked by locomotives – the S&DR was still using the horse-drawn stage coaches and only introduced the first steam powered service in December 1830. The engine was offered for sale in 1839, but was never scrapped, and is now on display in Canterbury.

The next class developed by Robert Stephenson at the Newcastle works incorporated more new features, and is known as the Planet class. The first two engines introduced in 1831 were *Samson* and *Goliath* which, though not exactly giants by modern standards, were large for the time at 10 tons. The most obvious difference when looking at the engine is the outside frame, made up of a sandwich of a timber beam, with iron on either side. The beams were set outside the wheels, leaving plenty of space for the horizontal cylinders to be placed under the boiler, bolted to the firebox and driving a crank axle. The engine had a 2-2-0 wheel arrangement, with 5ft diameter drive wheels, though later versions were also built as 0-4-0s. Another new feature was the dome above the boiler, in which steam was collected before reaching the cylinders, helping to keep it dry. Forging cranked axles tended to be something of a problem at first, and there were problems with breakages. Stephenson made allowances for this by having subframes inside the wheels with extra bearings for the cranked axle. If the worst happened and the axle broke, the wheels would still stay on the track. The engine was sprung and was generally agreed to give a smoother ride than its predecessors.

A replica has been built and is regularly steamed from the original Manchester terminus, Liverpool Road station, now

part of the Manchester Museum of Science and Industry. Seeing it in action, the most striking, and slightly alarming feature is a pair of handles, rocking backwards and forwards on the footplate. This is, in fact, part of the valve gear mechanism. The system, as on *Rocket*, uses slip eccentrics. The two long eccentric rods pass between the cylinders and end in gabs, notches, near the valves. These engage with a rocking shaft that works the valve gear itself. The system is operated by means of the two levers that can be seen next to the driver, and because of the constant movement of the rocking shaft, these rods move as the engine travels along. Operating them is a complex business, involving both the levers and a foot pedal.

A replica of the Liverpool & Manchester Planet class, designed by Robert Stephenson, which is regularly steamed from the site of the former Liverpool Road station in Manchester.

One visitor to the Newcastle works was Robert L. Stevens. He already had an impressive record in using steam power. He and his father, Colonel John Stevens, had built the steamer *Phoenix*, the first to brave the Atlantic, with a voyage from New York, south down the coast to the Delaware River. He was President of the Camden & Amboy Rail Road & Transportation Co., founded in 1830, that planned to use a mixture of canal, river and rail transport to link New York to Philadelphia. He was sufficiently impressed by what he saw of the Planet engines to order one for the line. It was shipped over in sections and reassembled in New York. There was one slight adaptation, in that the American track was 4ft 10in gauge. It was an 0-4-0 engine, which proved problematic. Early American routes were generally engineered to follow the contours of the land to avoid extensive earthworks, a practice that often resulted in some quite extravagant curves that the engine found difficult to negotiate. By 1833, it was uncoupled and re-emerged as a 2-2-0. At a later date, a two wheeled truck was added at the front, making it into what was then a completely novel engine – a 2+2-2-0. A cow catcher was then stuck on the front of that and the footplate was given a cab, resulting in what looked like a hybrid Anglo-American engine. Originally it was prosaically named simply No.1, but later renamed *John Bull*. It was finally retired in the 1860s but was preserved for posterity and is now in the National Museum of American History in Washington DC.

It was not only in America that the Planets proved popular. Belgium was a comparatively new country, having separated from the Netherlands. Both George and Robert Stephenson visited the country to advise on the route for a line from Brussels to Ghent – work for which King Leopold awarded George the Order of Leopold. Two engines were delivered, one named *Flèche* and the other *Stephenson*. The route was opened from Brussels to Mechelen in May 1835, with a grand

ceremony to which both of the Stephensons were invited. A third engine, *L'Eléphant,* had by then been added to the stock.

John Bull, built for the American railroad company, Camden & Amboy. Basically it is a Planet-type locomotive with a two-wheel truck added. It is now preserved in Washington DC.

In the meantime, Stephenson was working on a larger version of the Planet class. The new engines had a 2-2-2 wheel arrangement, and the addition of the pair of trailing wheels allowed a larger firebox to be used. The class were known as the Patentees, after the first of the class. One notable example was built for the Bayerische Ludwigbahn named after King Ludwig, suggesting a rather grand affair, but, in fact, it was a very modest line, running from

Nurenberg to Fürth, just 10km away. A request for engines was sent to Newcastle, but when the reply came back, the Germans declared the price was too high and asked a local manufacturer to build an engine instead. That proved to be a complete failure, so they had to turn to Robert Stephenson after all. The engine was a Patentee type, built in 1835 and named *Adler* (Eagle). A replica has been built for the railway museum in Nuremberg and is regularly steamed. In 1837, the company built an even larger engine for the Versailles Railway, *La Victorieuse* with an 0-4-2 arrangement, and the largest cylinders yet seen on a locomotive, at 15in diameter and 18in stroke. It tipped the scales at 13 tons, a huge increase over *Adler*'s 8 tons.

Obviously, the works were very busy, and this is a good point to pause in the story of the locomotives to take a look at what the works themselves were like at this time. We have a first-hand account from Geroge Bruce who described the situation when he came to Newcastle as an apprentice in 1837. He was to go on to enjoy a distinguished career, becoming President of the Institution of Civil Engineers. At that time there were around 400 working at Forth Street and that year 29 locomotives left the works, which is extraordinary given the following account of the facilities:

> In 1837 there were no small planing or shaping machines: there was only one slotting machine, the use of which was very restricted. Wheels were driven onto their axles by sledge hammers wielded by strong arms alone. Steam hammers were, of course, unknown, and only hand labour was available for the ordinary work of the smith's shop and boiler yard, with the exception of the punching and shearing machinery. Riveting by machinery was unknown. It is scarcely credible, but it is a fact, that there was not a single crane in Robert Stephenson's shop in 1837. There were sheer-legs in the yard, by which a boiler could be lifted

> onto a truck and there were portable sheer-legs in the shop, by the skilful manipulation of which, at no little risk to life and limb, wonders were done in the way of transmitting heavy loads from one part of the shop to another.

One of the interesting points was the mention of just the one slotting machine of restricted use. That must have been very frustrating, for cutting slots in items such as piston rods and connecting rods by hand was a long and tedious affair. First a line of holes was drilled through the metal component, which were then turned into a rough slot by chipping away at the metal between the holes with a chisel. When that was completed, it had to be carefully filed to the correct dimensions. For anyone visiting the works, the main experience would have been of a cacophony of noise, dominated by the beating of metal on metal. If it all seems a little crude, it is worth noting that sales of locomotives that year brought in roughly £40,000, the equivalent of £5.5 million today. The steam hammer mentioned was not available, simply because it was not invented until 1839 – after which it was to become a vital tool in engineering workshops.

Among the customers for Patentees was the New Orleans Railroad. America at the time had a variety of different gauges, including 5ft 6in, known as the 'Texas gauge', because it was compulsory there. The order was never completed, but one man who worked on it was Daniel Gooch, who later wrote, 'I was much delighted in having so much room to arrange the engine.' In 1833, Brunel had just been appointed chief engineer for what would become the Great Western Railway (GWR) and had famously decided that the Stephenson gauge was simply too narrow for comfortable, fast trains, so the railway between Bristol and London would be 7ft gauge. Whatever his other merits, Brunel was not a brilliant mechanical engineer. The company at that time had no manufacturing capabilities, so he had to look to other manufacturers, who were presented with a major problem. Brunel insisted that piston speeds should not exceed 280ft per minute, though other engines were at that time working perfectly well with far higher speeds. He also limited engine weight to 8 tons for a four-wheeled engine. Orders went to Hawthorns of Newcastle, who tried to solve the weight problem by having the boiler mounted on a separate carriage, connected to the power unit by flexible pipes. They were not a success, but in 1837 Gooch had been appointed as Superintendent of Locomotives, and remembering the New Orleans engines, put in an order for a broad gauge Patentee engine. The engine was *North Star* that proved to be highly satisfactory. On an initial run with a 45 ton load, it achieved a speed of almost 40mph.

The Patentees were successful, but Stephenson was not altogether happy with the performance. There was a tendency for fireboxes to overheat, simply because the boilers were not big enough to absorb enough heat. He did not want to increase the diameter of the boiler, so extended the length instead. To do this he placed all six wheels under the boiler, leaving the firebox overhanging at the back. There were further modifications that included placing a single plate frame inside the wheels and placing the cylinders outside, doing away with the need for a cranked axle. The engines were very successful and examples were sent to France for the Marseilles & Avignon and Paris-Orleans railways. One of these, *L'Aigle*, built in 1846, is now preserved at the railway museum in Mulhouse. Engines of this type were to be used on French railways for many years.

The Stephensons were to face a new challenge in 1845. Once the GWR had acquired its own locomotive works at Swindon, Gooch was able to design his own engines. As the network spread, the disadvantages of having two gauges for mainline travel in a comparatively small country became evident. The result was the battle of the gauges – which would prevail,

A replica of the GWR broad-gauge locomotive *North Star* at Swindon.

the Stephenson or the Brunel? Gauge Commissioners were appointed to decide the issue and most of the expert witnesses they called favoured the narrower gauge, at which point Brunel, who had always been convinced his system was the better for fast running, suggested a trial in which equivalent engines would run over a similar track to see which produced the best performance. The GWR were represented by one of the Firefly class, *Ixion,* and the Stephenson camp by a long boiler locomotive. The former achieved a speed of 60mph and the latter just 53mph. In truth, it proved nothing – there was no way of telling whether the difference was due to the track or the engines. In any case, with 1,900 miles of Stephenson gauge already built, it was inevitable that the broad gauge would lose out. The Stephenson works could continue to concentrate on producing what were now officially standard gauge locomotives.

One area of locomotive development that changed considerably in the early years was valve gear. In the 1830s, the slip eccentrics gave way to fixed eccentrics, in which usually x-shaped gabs engaged with pins to raise and lower them. It was not an ideal arrangement and reversing often proved quite difficult. A 'gentleman apprentice' (one whose father paid for his training), William Williams, was training as a draughtsman at Forth Street. In 1841, he began thinking of ways in which the system could be improved. He came up with the idea of having one end of the valve rod moving up or down a slotted link, to connect either the forward or backward eccentric rod. This was not merely an improvement on the previous system but was fundamentally different. The engine was no longer controlled through an either/or system, full forward or full reverse, but could be smoothly adjusted to in-between positions. This meant that it was possible to vary the cut-off point at which steam could be admitted to the cylinder. When starting up, for example, steam could be allowed in for the full travel of the piston, but when up to speed, the cut-off point could be earlier in the stroke, allowing the steam to continue to expand. This could easily be controlled by the reversing gear on the footplate. It made for much greater efficiency in running – one could compare it with a car, starting in first gear and moving up to top gear as it gained speed.

The new design was sent to Robert Stephenson who responded with enthusiasm. 'At the first blush it is very satisfactory and I sincerely hope on a more mature investigation it will prove really so ... If it answers it will be worth a Jew's eye and the contriver of it should be rewarded.' It was successfully fitted to a 2-4-0 locomotive in 1842, but there was controversy over who should get the credit as Williams had involved a pattern maker, William Howe. This has never really been settled and it probably safest to share the credit between them. But whoever was ultimately responsible, the arrival of the new gear gave engine drivers far greater control over how the engine was run and greatly improved its efficiency. It is because of the use of variable cut-offs that rail enthusiasts can often be found on steam trains by an open window, listening to the changing pattern of the puffing engine and seeing in their mind's eye just how the driver is adjusting his controls.

The Newcastle works were not only producing engines to their own designs, but were quite happy to take on ideas developed by others. One of these designers was Thomas Russell Crampton, who after a conventional apprenticeship, went to work as an assistant to Daniel Gooch. He was well aware that one way to achieve greater speeds was to have large drive wheels. There was a problem, however, if the axle was fitted below the boiler in the conventional manner. That raised the centre of gravity of the engine and could make for instability. His solution was to move the axle to a point beneath a raised firebox and have the boiler lowered. Crampton locomotives were built with drive wheels up to 8ft in diameter. Stephenson built a number of Crampton type engines for the South Eastern and the London, Chatham & Dover Railways.

Providing locomotives for overseas railways was an important part of the business. The first line to be built in Africa was closely tied to the need for good communications between Britain and India. There were two alternatives; either take the long sea voyage round the southern tip of Africa or leave a ship at Alexandria and go across land to Suez, a port on the Red Sea. The P&O Company had horse-drawn carriages for passengers and 3,000 camels for freight. The advantages of a railway were obvious, but negotiations on who should build such a line were protracted and it was only in 1851 that the Khedive Abbas I gave his permission for a line from Cairo to Alexandria that would later be extended to Suez. The engineer in charge of construction was Robert Stephenson, so it was inevitable that when the line was built, orders for locomotives would come from Forth Street. The first engine to be delivered was a conventional 2-4-0 locomotive, and other engines would be delivered over the years. None, however, was as bizarre as the special locomotive intended for the sole use of the Khedive's Train of 1862, which was to take him between his various palaces. It is a riot of decoration designed by Matthew Digby Wyatt, an architect best known for his work in designing Paddington station with Brunel. What Robert Stephenson himself would have thought of it we will never know, for he had died in 1859. In his time, he had supervised a pioneering works that had had profound effect on railway development around the world.

The company continued to thrive after Robert's death, and among the many locomotives that they built were some that were notable for various reasons, one of which was the experimental engine, known as 'Fowler's Ghost'. Sir John Fowler was chief engineer for the newly formed Metropolitan Railway, authorised in 1854 to link the London main line stations of Paddington and King's Cross to the City. It was partly in deep cuttings, but much of it was also underground, in tunnels constructed on the cut-and-cover principle. There was an obvious problem with smoke and fumes in what was, in effect, the first underground railway. It was agreed that the

This remarkably ornate locomotive was specially built for the use of the Khedive on the line from Cairo to Alexandria.

line should be available for both broad and standard gauge engines, and Fowler designed a broad gauge locomotive that he hoped would solve the problem. Outwardly, it was a conventional locomotive, but the difference lay inside the boiler. There was a conventional firebox behind the trailing axle, but most of the boiler consisted of a long 'combustion chamber' filled with bricks. The fire was used when the engine was outside the underground section to heat the bricks to a point where they were incandescent and would then be hot enough to provide all the heat necessary for a run on the underground section. The exhaust steam, instead of being allowed to escape into the atmosphere was passed into a condenser. It had its nickname from the fact that it was almost silent when running. It was built at Forth Street in 1862 but was not a success – the heat from the combustion chamber could not be controlled and there were genuine fears

A slightly faded photograph of 'Fowler's Ghost', designed for use on the Metropolitan Railway underground sections.

of bursting the boiler. The answer was later found in more conventional condensing engines.

Foreign orders continued to be important, particularly as so many British companies now had their own locomotive works. Robert Stephenson had been the engineer for the first public railway in Norway, the Trunk Railway that ran between Oslo and Eidsvold, so it was inevitable that the works would supply the first locomotives, when the line opened in 1854. They were 2-4-0 locomotives and one of the later Norwegian engines, Class 2a *Caroline* built in 1861 remained in service until 1920 and is now preserved in the national railway museum, still operational. Scandinavia provided a useful market for the Newcastle company. In 1862 they built twenty-four locomotives for the opening of the Danish line from Aarhus to Randers. These proved to be remarkably durable. The last was not withdrawn from service until 1935 and one of these splendid 0-4-2 engines clocked

Norwegian Trunk Railway Class A locomotive, crossing a rather alarming looking wooden bridge near Eidsvoll.

up an astonishing 1,149,500 miles of service, before being retired for a well-earned rest in the Danish National Railway Museum. They were to go on to manufacture engines not only for other European countries but for countries on all five continents.

This was a period that saw the works turning out some impressively large engines. The first locomotives the company had built for use in Africa were their modest locomotives for Egypt. When railways were developed in southern Africa, the demand was for more powerful locomotives. The Natal Government Railway that was authorised in 1875 ordered impressive 4-6-0 engines and later in 1896 even grander 4-6-4s.

Australia was also a valuable customer from the 1850s with the opening of the South Australian Railway. Other imposing engines of the time included 2-6-0s for Central Uruguay and 4-6-2s for the Bengal Nagpur Railway. By the end of the century, the company had constructed around 30,000 locomotives but was about to enter a new phase. In 1889 a public company was established, Robert Stephenson & Co. Ltd. By now it had outgrown the Forth Street works and there was no land available for expansion, so a new works was established in Darlington that was completed in 1902. International orders remained vital and the demand for large engines continued to grow. The Bengal Nagpur Railway ordered a 2-8-0 engine in 1903 that proved immensely satisfactory, and it became the standard type for Indian State Railways. The Bengal company also ordered some imposing 2-8-2 tank engines. The grandest engine of this period was probably the 2-10-0 supplied for the 5ft 6in gauge Great Western Railway of Argentina – it weighed in at nearly 80 tons without the tender. As well as supplying powerful engines for the South America broad gauge, they also supplied equally impressive 4-8-2s for the South African 3ft 6in gauge lines.

The outbreak of war in 1914 brought yet more changes. From 1916 the company was entirely given over to manufacturing munitions until the following year when the War Ministry began to order locomotives to be sent to mainland Europe. Altogether, eighty-two 2-8-0s were built and thirty 0-6-0 tank engines for the 3ft 6in gauge, with production continuing up to 1920. The following years saw production fall as the world experienced an economic depression. In 1937, the company bought the locomotive department of Hawthorns to form Robert Stephenson & Hawthorns Ltd, with the idea of concentrating production of industrial locomotives at the Hawthorns work in Newcastle and passenger locomotives at Darlington. The story of the new company will be continued in Chapter 4, following the history of Hawthorn.

A 4-6-0 locomotive, built c.1885 for the Australian Glenelg Railway Company.

Chapter Three

The Vulcan Foundry

The works were built at Newton-le-Willows in 1830 by Liverpool engineer Charles Tayleur, originally with the idea of supplying metalwork for the L&MR. They were built next to the main line and had their own rail connection. Robert Stephenson became a partner in the firm in 1832 but seems to have resigned after just a couple of years, presumably due to the heavy demands of running Forth Street and a possible conflict of interest. The first locomotives were ordered in 1832, but not for the L&MR. The order came from John Hargreaves, who at the time ran a fleet of boats from a site on the Bridgewater Canal. It was not normal practice for canal companies, who owned a waterway, to run their own boats. Instead, they collected tolls from users such as Hargreaves. The same system was now applied to the North Union Railway that was to link the L&MR at Parkhead to Bolton, with Hargreaves being granted a licence to run trains on the route. He ordered two locomotives from Vulcan, that were named *Tayleur* and *Stephenson*, both of which were very similar to Stephenson's Planet class, with inside cylinders. The main difference from the Planets was that the wheels were coupled in an 0-4-0 arrangement. Two more Planet class type engine were built at much the same time for the Warrington & Newton Railway, but this time with a 2-2-0 formation and the drive wheels increased in diameter from 4ft 8in to 5ft.

As the works were being established, there was an urgent need for housing for the increasingly large workforce. The company acquired land, probably in 1833, and built what became known as Vulcan Village. It consisted of 114 houses

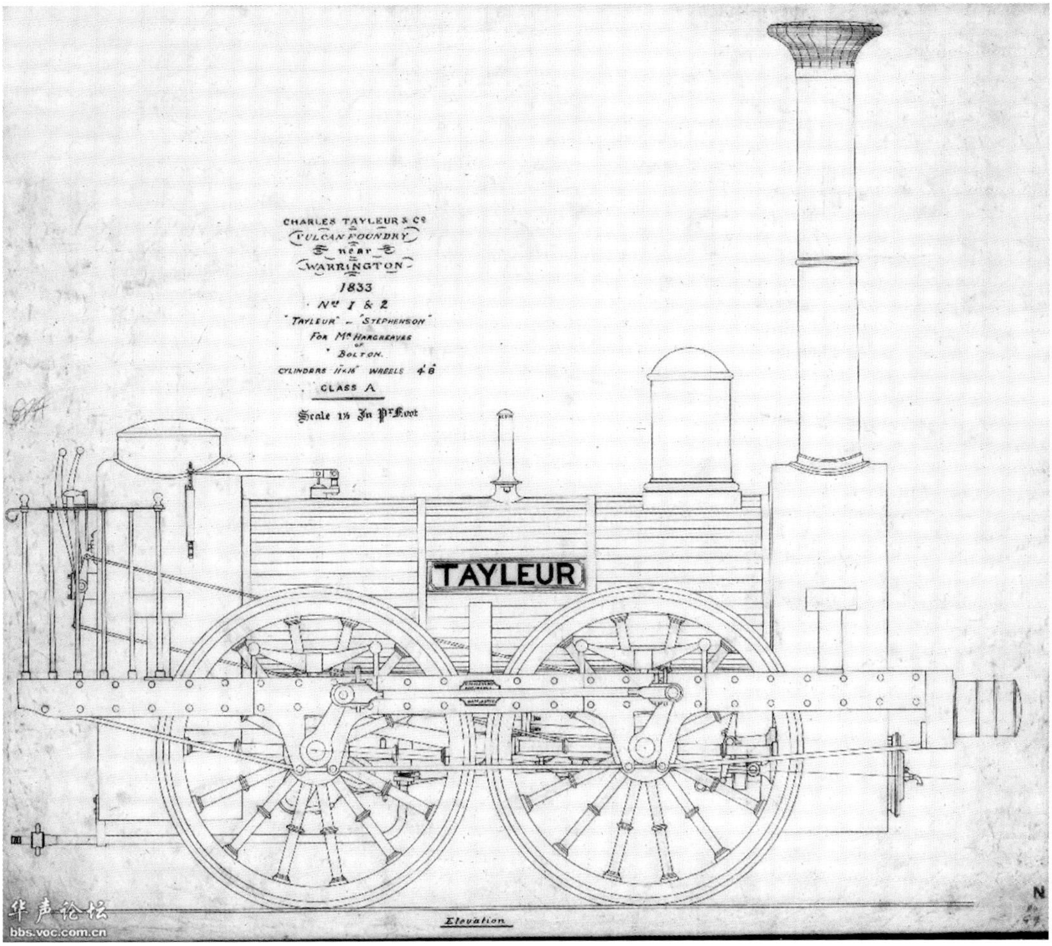

One of the two locomotives supplied by Charles Tayleur for the North Union Railway in 1832.

arranged as six rows of terraces with a green space in the middle. Later, a church and school were added, and eventually the green was built on to provide the Vulcan Inn and a washhouse. It would seem that it was a popular place to work as many generations followed each other into the Foundry – one such family, the Harrisons, traced their connection right back to the first member joining in 1840. And once joined, few seem to have left – John Edwards first turned up for work when Victoria was on the throne and only retired in 1946 at the age of 79. Among those who came to work at the foundry as an apprentice was Daniel Gooch.

The company soon began receiving overseas orders, including engines for two early American railroads, the Philadelphia and Colombia and the South Carolina, which were all 4-2-0s with the leading wheels mounted on a bogie, the first of their kind. The South Carolina Railroad had initially had a locomotive the *Best Friend of Charleson* built for them in 1830 at the West Point Foundry, the first American built locomotive to go into service. It was a curious affair with a vertical boiler which tragically blew up, killing the crew. The order for three engines from Vulcan came in 1835. Another American order followed, this time for the Raleigh & Gaston Railroad in North Carolina. At roughly the same time, eight 2-2-2s were built for the Paris & St. Germaine Railway, a line which did not quite reach its destination of St-Germain-en-Laye on the outskirts of Paris as locomotives were unable to cope with the steep hill on the final section. The terminus was at Le Pecq. The company provided one of the half dozen first locomotives to be sent to Russia for use on the line from St. Petersburg to Pavlosk, passing through Tsarskoye Selo, which was the original terminus for locomotives – the section for which Timothy Hackworth had supplied an engine. Other locomotives were built at this time for the Kaiser Ferdinand Nordbahn, a line built to link Vienna to salt mines near Krakow. Two 0-4-2 goods locomotives were sent out to work the first section that opened in 1837 to Floridsdork on the outskirts of Vienna. It never, in fact, reached Krakow. Another 0-4-2 went to the Belgian State Railway in 1835.

This was a busy period for the works and, not surprisingly given his role as a partner, designs were strongly influenced by Robert Stephenson and his developing ideas as described in the previous chapter. Export orders were of great importance to the company, and would remain so, but there were also important local orders as well. The company supplied a 2-2-0 for the opening of London's very first railway, the London & Greenwich. The GWR ordered three locomotives for their broad gauge line in 1837, all of which had to satisfy Brunel's requirements that included comparatively slow piston speeds and a light weight, which certainly produced headaches for the builders. The locomotives were *Vulcan*, *Aeolus* and *Bacchus*, all of which were 2-2-2s with 8ft diameter drive wheels and 14in cylinders. *Vulcan* was the first to be tried on 28 December 1837, but it was never very satisfactory, not surprisingly, being underpowered. It was withdrawn in 1843 and rebuilt as a 2-2-2T tank engine, with new 6ft drive wheels. In that form, it continued in service until 1863. The other engines in the group suffered similar fates, as did the next three engines delivered to the GWR, which were slightly different, having 12in cylinders. Once Daniel Gooch took over at the GWR Swindon works, a whole new generation of vastly improved broad gauge locomotives were built there to his design.

By the end of the 1830s, Stephenson had left the company and Charles Tayleur Jnr. had taken over from his father. Henry Dübs was appointed works manager, and we shall meet him again later. From the middle of the 1840s, the company was kept busy with orders for engines from all over Britain, from the Scottish Central Railway to the Vale of Neath Railway. One important commission was for a comparatively minor line, the Waterford & Kilkenny. In 1846, Vulcan built the world's first side tank engine for them. The following year, the name of the company was changed to the Vulcan Foundry Company.

Arguably the most important contract received in these years was for locomotives for the Great India Peninsula Railway, not actually all that great since it was only intended to run for just 30 miles from Bombay (Mumbai) to Kalyan. There had been a great deal of discussion about whether to adopt the Stephenson gauge or Brunel's broad gauge and eventually a compromise was reached and 5ft 6in was adopted. It seemed a logical decision and was intended to be the standard gauge for the whole of India, but within just a few years economy became more important than standardisation and a 1m gauge network began to appear, followed later by narrow gauge lines in the hills. In 1851 an order was placed with Vulcan for six 2-4-0s with inside cylinders and 5ft diameter drive wheels. They arrived in India the following year and three of them, *Sultan*, *Sindh* and *Sahib*, were used for the official opening of the line in April 1853. It had not yet reached Kalyan but stopped at Thale. The train of 14 carriages and around 400 passengers covered the 21 miles at a stately speed of 20mph. This was just the beginning of what was to prove a valuable partnership in which many more locomotives would leave England for the subcontinent, eventually supplying 2,750 locomotives at the rate of one a fortnight.

The beginning of the twentieth century saw a vastly increased demand for locomotives for India, and it was decided

Standard Passenger 4-4-0 tender locomotive, built in 1911 for the Indian North Western Railway, now in the Museum of Science and Industry, Manchester.

to try to introduce standard models. The British Engineering Standards Association suggested among other classes that there should be an 0-6-0 standard goods locomotive, the SG class. They had inside cylinders and 5ft 6in drive wheels. In later versions, a superheater was added to create the SGS Class. They first appeared in 1903 and proved to be highly successful engines which were frequently used on passenger as well as goods trains. Over the years, Vulcan built 552 SG Class and 362 SGS Class – many of the former would later have superheaters fitted as well. The standard passenger (SPS) differed from the SGS mainly in the wheel arrangement, as 4-4-0s. Among the later developments was a series of Pacific 4-6-2 engines, all with the prefix X, the first of which was the XA Class. The first of 113 engines in this class was built in 1929. Another important group featured side tank engines, beginning with the WM Class of 1942, all 2-6-4Ts, the first thirty of which were built at Vulcan.

When I visited India in the early 1980s, Delhi was still being served by steam locomotives, but elsewhere in the country electrification was already well established. As early as 1928, Vulcan had built a locomotive, in conjunction with Swiss Locomotive and Machine Works, designed to take direct current at 1.5 kilovolts from overhead wires via a pantograph. At each end of the locomotive was a four-wheeled bogie, with three of the four wheels connected. The Class was known as WCG and altogether forty-one engines were constructed. The engine was especially useful on the line from Mumbai to Poona (Pone). The first line out of Bombay had hugged the coast, but to move inland it had to climb the Western Ghats, the cliffs that rose to a height of 2,500 feet. To do this, the line had to zigzag up the cliff – the works involved were immense. The line up the Bhore Ghat had a total rise of 2,000ft, included 25 tunnels and 22 bridges and had a maximum gradient of 1 in 37. This was the line on which WCG1 did sterling service. The engine is now preserved in the Delhi railway museum.

The company continued to develop and supply electric locomotives into the 1950s. Vulcan also provided locomotives for nearby Sri Lanka over a long period of time. Appropriately, the 4,000th locomotive to be built at Vulcan was a 4-6-0 for the 5ft 6in East Indian Railway, a suitably imposing engine.

Japan was comparatively late in acquiring a railway system and the first line, from Tokyo to Kyoto, had to be built through a difficult terrain of mountains and river valleys liable to flooding. It was decided that a 3ft 6in gauge would be appropriate for coping with the many tight curves that would be necessary. The first section to be completed ran from Yedo to Yokohama and was opened in 1872 by the Mikado, with a 2-4-0 tank engine supplied by Vulcan. Railways were such a novelty that the invited guests treated the carriages as if they were entering a neighbour's house and took their shoes off. There was considerable consternation when the train reached the far end and they discovered their shoes had not followed them on the journey. More locomotives were to be sent over

Japanese Railway 150 SL, supplied by Vulcan in 1871.

the years. China was also to order locomotives, including the most impressive, built for the Guangdong to Hankou railway, which featured some severe gradients. In 1935, the first of the 4-8-4 KF Class was delivered, and twenty-four of the class were built. One of these mighty engines is now in the National Railway Museum in York.

Over the years, Vulcan were to supply steam engines to every continent. Among them were some remarkable engines. We in Britain tend to associate the famous double Fairlie engines with the Ffestiniog Railway, but they were in fact used all over the world, and examples were built by Vulcan for the Dunedin & Port Chalmers Railway in New Zealand in 1872 and for the Denver & Rio Grande in America the following year. Other customers included Mexico, who ordered several engines and Vulcan-built Fairlies appeared in countries as far apart as Portugal and Peru.

The Central South African Railway was opened in 1902. The route from Johannesburg to Kamatipoort contained a steep section between Waterval Onder and Waterval Boven

Fairley doubles are associated with the Ffestiniog Railway, but this example, *Josephine* was supplied to the Dunedin and Port Chalmers Railway in New Zealand in 1872.

that was operated by a rack railway system. In 1905, the company ordered two 4-6-4T rack engines from Vulcan and when the specifications arrived, the British engineers felt they could improve on the system. The original had called for two 400mm cylinders with a 630mm stroke, roughly 19in by 25in. The new engine had four cylinders, the two outside coupled to the drive wheels were reduced to 18in with a 20in stroke, and two smaller inside cylinders were used to drive the cogs that worked with the ladder rack. Two engines were delivered, but in the event, they proved unsatisfactory, mainly because the boiler proved inadequate for four cylinders, and the engines often slipped. The rack mechanism was removed and the engines remained in use as conventional tank engines. It was not Vulcan's finest hour.

The two world wars inevitably brought great changes. In the years from 1914-18, the works were almost entirely given over to the manufacture of munitions. There was a similar situation at the start of the Second World War, when a lot of the work involved building 'Matilda' tanks. In 1943,

Central South African rack railway locomotive No. 995.

however, the Ministry of Supply started ordering 'Austerity' 2-8-0 locomotives. These were based on the LMS 8F Class locomotives, a freight version of the famous Stanier 'Black Fives'. Three hundred and ninety had been built by 1935. Fifty sturdy 0-6-0s were also built for shunting duties. At the end of the war, as part of the work of rehabilitation of Eastern Europe, they began producing what were known as the Liberation Class of heavy freight 2-8-0s, all built to the continental loading gauge. Altogether, 120 were built and sent to Luxemburg, Poland, Yugoslavia and Czechoslovakia.

In 1944, the company took over Robert Stephenson and although they continued to manufacture steam locomotives, they also began building diesels and diesel-electrics in conjunction with English Electric. The most imposing engines produced in the 1940s, were the 4-8-0 Class 15B engines for the Buenos Aires Great Southern Railways 5ft 6in gauge line. They weighed in at a massive 148½ tons with tender. In 1955, English Electric took over the whole company, and the very last of 6,204 steam locomotives that had been built at Vulcan rolled out of Newton-le-Willows in 1956, a 4-8-4 Class 31 for East African Railways. The Vulcan Foundry continued in

Chinese KF Class 4-8-4 of 1935 at the National Railway Museum, York.

operation, but to understand how it developed, we need to take a look back to the work of the English Electric Company that took it over.

English Electric was formed immediately after the First World War in 1918, from a number of companies that had been involved in different aspects of war work, providing everything from steam turbines to aircraft. They began

The last steam engine to be built at the Vulcan Foundry in 1956: a 4-8-4 Class 31 for East African Railway.

manufacturing locomotives in 1923, with an order from the 3ft 6in gauge Midland Railway of New Zealand. It ran from Christchurch through the Southern Alps to the opposite coast. This involved the construction of a tunnel between Otira and Arthur's Pass, over five miles long and with a gradient for most of its length of 1:33. It was decided that using steam locomotives would be too dangerous, because of the likely build up of gases, so the tunnel was electrified, with a small coal-fired power station providing the electricity at 1,500 volts DC. Six locomotives of what became the EO Class were built at the English Electric works in Preston, the first of which, E1, was a battery electric, while the other five were conventional electric locomotives with pantographs connecting to the overhead supply. They were Bo-Bo engines, that is they were carried on two sets of four wheeled bogies. Between 1924 and 1926, they built six similar but larger versions of the EO Class for the Harbour Commissioners of Montreal, Canada, four of which were still running in 1995.

In 1936, the company began building diesel engines at Preston. A new departure for the company came in 1938, when they built DM Multiple units for the line linking Wellington, New Zealand to the northern suburb of Johnsonville. They would continue to provide similar multiple units as the Wellington electrified system expanded. The outbreak of war in 1939 saw English Electric, like many other engineering firms, devoting their resources to the military effort. The end of the war brought English Electric a lot of work for the newly nationalised British Rail, at first providing engines for a variety of diesel shunters. The move to the Vulcan Foundry brought a new impetus to the company's railway work. In 1958 they began building the Class 40 diesel-electric locomotives. The diesel engine was used to drive a generator to provide the power for the electric motor. By 1962, they had supplied forty of these engines, and later modifications appeared. The most important change came in 1965, when they began work on the Class 55 engines, better known as 'Deltics'. The name derives from the engine, in which three cylinders are arranged in a triangle, a design first developed by Napier's for use in naval craft. They were at the time the most powerful single-unit diesel-electrics in the world with a power rating of 3,300hp and capable of speeds in excess of 100mph. The prototype D1 looked more American than British, with a blue livery, featuring decorative yellow designs down the sides and a yellow chevron on the nose. It has been preserved as part of the national collection.

In 1961, the company developed an experimental locomotive with a gas turbine engine, which although it was successful in trials, never went into production. Two new types were built in the period 1965-6. Class 73 was an electro-diesel, specifically designed to run on the electrified Southern

The inaugural run of the DMU at Wellington, New Zealand in 1938.

Region section of the network, where electricity was supplied by a third rail, as on the London Underground, instead of by overhead cables. It could, however, also be used with just the diesel motor when operating on other parts of the system. Classes 83 and 86 were electric locomotives, built for the newly electrified West Coast main line. They were intended to set the standard for future development of electrification. During this period, the company was also kept busy with orders for diesel, diesel-electric and electric locomotives for Australia, Tasmania, New Zealand and Africa. Locomotive manufacture ended in 1970. The works had been turning out a huge variety of locomotives, not just for Britain, but for countries all round the world.

CHAPTER FOUR

The Leeds Companies

If one thinks about towns specially associated with locomotive construction, names such as Swindon and Crewe are the first that come to mind, but Leeds was home to five companies. Fenton, Murray & Wood have a special place in railway history as builders of the engines for the Middleton Colliery Railway. The works, the Round Foundry, named after the rotunda that formed part of the complex, in the Holbeck district were completed in 1797. Following Trevithick's pioneering work in developing the locomotive, there was a hiatus as, although the engines were successful, they tended to crack the brittle, cast iron rails. The Napoleonic Wars created many problems, among which was providing fodder for the horses that were used to carry coal from the colliery to the Aire & Calder Navigation. The colliery agent, John Blenkinsop approached Matthew Murray with a suggestion that a system could be made to work by using a rack rail, connecting with cogs on the engine, which would give extra traction for a light engine. One important aspect of the engine was the use of accurately machined slide valves, thanks to Murray's own invention of a planing machine, capable of producing a flat surface. The result was a success, and caused much interest among other colliery owners, one of whom sent his engine man, George Stephenson, to look at this new device. He, of course, went on to build his first colliery engine, using many of the features found on the Middleton engine.

The Leeds company built two engines for the Midleton Colliery in 1812 and two more the following year. They also supplied two other rack engines to the Kenton & Coxlodge Colliery near Newcastle in 1813. What is less well known is that, after a long pause, they began building conventional locomotives in 1831 under a new name, Fenton, Murray & Jackson and continued in business until 1842, during which time they built over seventy engines.

Ironically, since the company had earlier refused to build a locomotive for the S&DR, they now found themselves in the position of building for the Robert Stephenson company, who had more orders than they could handle. These were mostly standard Planet and Patentee Class engines. Another important customer was the GWR. When Daniel Gooch began designing locomotives, the GWR had not yet acquired its own locomotive works. In 1840, he introduced the famous Firefly Class of 2-2-2 engines, with 7ft drive wheels and the domed firebox in a style that became known as Gothic. The first of the class, *Fire Fly* was recorded at a very respectable 58mph with three vehicles in tow. Many different builders were used and the Leeds company provided twenty engines. Less well known is the Leo class, developed for the less romantic goods traffic. These were 2-4-0s with 5ft drive wheels, the first GWR engines to have coupled wheels. Just three were built – *Hecla, Stromboli and Etna*. Gooch rated the company very highly. Other important commissions were for the H&SR, the Leeds & Selby and the North Midland.

There were also a number of engines sent overseas, starting with a locomotive for Russia in 1831and two the following year for the Roanes Andrézieux Railway, the first public railway in France, opened in 1827, originally worked by horses. In 1834 they supplied an engine for the South Carolina Railroad. Because the track was laid with timber rails topped with a continuous iron strip, speeds on the line were limited to 25mph and passengers travelling the 157 mile route between Charleston and Hamburg faced a nine-hour journey. Other lines supplied were the Munich & Augsburg, the Montpelier & Cette and the Paris & Versailles in 1838, and the Paris Orleans in 1840; all were 2-2-2s. In 1843, with no more orders coming in, the company was closed down. Some of the buildings had survived, but not unfortunately the rotunda. They now form the Round Foundry Media Centre.

There is a connection between the Round Foundry and our next company that began as Todd, Kitson & Laird: James Todd had worked for Matthew Murray and was the only one of the three original partners with experience of locomotive building. James Kitson was born in 1807 in a tavern kept by a drunken father. He was apprenticed to a dye works, but set about self-education at the Leeds Mechanics' Institute, where he became fascinated by railway development. The third member, David Laird, was a rich farmer, who invested in the project hoping for a quick return and when that failed to materialise soon left. The company was formed in 1835 and was to change its name several time over the years, but by the 1860s had simply become Kitson & Co. That is the name that is best known, and which will be used from here on in.

The three partners took over a former woollen cloth mill and began construction with a freight engine, known at the time as a 'luggage engine', for the L&MR. This was an 0-4-2 designed by Robert Stephenson and John Melling that included the latter's radial valve gear and a firebox with water filled firebars. Its most notable feature was the copper 'haystack' firebox. Completed in 1838, it was named *Lion* and after completion it is said that a hole had to be knocked in the mill wall to get the engine out. There is a shadow of doubt whether this was actually *Lion* or an identical engine built for the North Lancashire, but *Lion* appears to be the more likely candidate. It was to be modified over the years but had a career that its builders could never have imagined. It reappeared in 1953 as the eponymous engine in the Ealing comedy *The Titfield Thunderbolt*. The old engine had another moment of glory in the cavalcade of locomotives that marked the 150th anniversary of the Rainhill Trials, held at Rainhill. *Rocket* was meant to lead the parade, but derailed at the start

***Lion* at** the Rainhill Cavalcade, staged to mark the 150th anniversary of the famous locomotive trials of 1829.

and *Lion* took the honour. It is now on display at the Museum of Liverpool.

The old mill was clearly unsatisfactory and in 1837 the company announced that they were going to build 'entirely new premises' in Hunslet, at what was to become the Airedale Foundry. In the 1840s they built a series of 0-6-0 locomotives, two for the H&SR, two for the Newcastle & Darlington and ten for the York & North Midland. But like many others, they were soon looking for export orders. Two 0-6-0 engines were supplied to the Belgian Eastern Junction Railway in 1855 and the following year two 2-4-0 went to the Grand Central Belge. A far more useful connection came with the first orders for India with thirty-five 0-4-2 and 2-2-2 well tanks, all built between 1855 and 1856. One of the latter was supplied to the 5ft 6in East India Railway Co and reached Calcutta (Kolkata) in 1855. An outside cylinder locomotive was originally simply known by its serial number 481, but in 1895 it was given a name, *The Fairy Queen*. It was preserved originally as a static exhibit, but then restored to working order. For a time, it was run regularly at the National Railway Museum in Delhi, where I had the pleasure of seeing it work. Then for a time it was out of service and it was discovered that several parts had to be entirely remade. It is now back in working order and steaming again, reputedly the oldest steam engine in the world still in regular service. Many other locomotives were built for India, including twenty built for the Great India Peninsula Railway in 1865-6. These were 0-8-0 tank engines mainly used as banking engines on the steep inclines of the Western Ghats.

The 1860s also proved to be a busy time with orders coming in from Russia, starting with fifteen 2-4-0s in 1869 for the Tamboff and Saratoff Railway, which led to a spate of orders in the early 1870s for other Russian lines over the next few years. A total of forty-one 0-6-0s were supplied to various companies in Russia in the early years of the decade. Nearer home, there were several orders from British companies, including the Midland Railway. They introduced their Class 700 double-frame 0-6-0 goods locomotives in 1869 and over the next five years, 316 engines were built. Several companies were involved, and Kitson was one of the major suppliers. These were highly successful and the last were only withdrawn from the Midland in 1905 and even then, that was not the end, for fifty were sold on to the Italian State Railway where they continued in steam into the 1920s. An order came from the Great Eastern Railway where Robert Sinclair had designed two classes of locomotives with 7ft 6in drive wheels. There were two versions: a 2-2-2 intended for goods traffic, but

occasionally used on passenger trains and a larger 4-2-2. Later, the line was to order ten 4-2-2s, designed by Massey Bromley, notable for their 7ft 6in drive wheels and 4ft bogie wheels. They first appeared in 1881 and looked splendid but were taken out of service after just a decade of use and broken up.

Kitson locomotive built for the Great Eastern Railway between 1862 and 1867.

A 2-8-0 Kitson locomotive built for the Great Eastern Railway c.1905, seen here in LNER livery at Retford in 1947.

Kitson not only built to designs supplied by the railway companies but were innovators themselves. They built a large number of industrial locomotives over the years, with distinctive tapered chimneys. Among the more interesting and successful ventures was the development of steam tram engines. The story begins in 1876 when they built three combined steam tramcars to a design by W.R. Rowan, but by 1878 they had started producing their own version with, at first, vertical boilers. Over the years they were to take out several patents, including for their own gear mechanism and an automatic braking device that cut in when a speed of more than 10mph was reached as that was the government speed limit for trams. Later versions were built with horizontal boilers. All were enclosed and the movement protected from grit and dust by metal plates. They were condensing engines, but quite unlike the more familiar Metropolitan Railway versions. Here the exhaust steam was condensed in copper tubes on the roof and the condensate passed down to the feedwater tank. A similar device was used in a more conventional locomotive supplied to a copper mine in South Africa, where the track of nearly 100 miles passed through a very, hot arid region. Altogether over 300 were built, the last appearing in 1901, by which time electric trams were starting to take over. One survivor is still at work. It was built in 1881 for the Christchurch Tramway Co. of New Zealand and is regularly steamed at the Ferrymead Heritage Park in New Zealand.

Overseas orders continued to be important and included twenty 2-4-0s for the Chemin de fer de l'Ouest in France and an even bigger order for Class C22 4-6-0s for the 1m gauge Cordoba Central Railway of Argentina in 1889. A total of sixty-nine reached Argentina, but seventy-four were built – five were lost at sea and replaced. In 1901 fourteen more, slightly heavier, engines were added as the C24 Class. In 1894 Kitson built the first of their Kitson-Meyer locomotives. These were a development from a type of locomotive originally

One of three Kitson condensing locomotives, based on their steam tram design, and supplied to the Cape Copper Co. South Africa, 1886-8.

designed by Wensel Günter in 1851, with two sets of drive wheels mounted on separate bogies. The idea was taken further by Jean-Jacques Mayer, who designed an 0-4-4-0 version in, for which he took out a patent. This was the basis for the Kitson-Meyer articulated engines. The first 0-6-6-0s were built for the 3ft 6in gauge Anglo-Chilean Nitrate and Railway Co. in 1894. There were to be different versions provided for countries around the world. Among the most challenging lines were those that crossed the Andes. The route from the Chilean coast at Antofagasta to La Paz in Bolivia, the FCAB Railway, started at sea level and ended at an altitude of 3,689m. It was originally built to a 2ft 6in gauge but converted to 1m gauge in the twentieth century. Kitson supplied the line with 2-6-6-2 engines. Even more demanding were the engines for the Trans Andine Argentine 1m gauge line, in which there were many sections, with gradients up to 17 per cent that were worked with the assistance of an Abt rack system. The line opened throughout in 1910, worked by Kitson-Meyer 0-8-6-0 locomotives. They were fitted with an extra cylinder to provide drive for the rack system, but this had to be abandoned as the boiler did not produce enough steam. Two of these locomotives are now preserved in Chile.

During the war years of 1914-18, they continued building locomotives for the government and for India. The post war years brought fewer orders and companies were beginning to look at diesel as an alternative to steam power. The company decided that there would be great advantages in combing the two. By using steam power to get the engine moving, designers would not have to worry about variable transmission for the diesel. In 1926 they began work on the hybrid engine for the LNER. There were four pairs of opposed cylinders, driving a crankshaft set between them. Oil was used to heat the boiler and the start was exactly the same as in a conventional locomotive. Once the engine had reached a speed of around 5mph, the steam was cut off and the diesel injectors took over. The waste heat was used to keep up boiler pressure, so that steam was available for the whistle, brakes and, if necessary, another start. The engine was a success in that it did the job satisfactorily, but the cost of diesel for a heavy locomotive made it uneconomic in comparison with a coal-fired locomotive. The experiment had cost Kitson a good deal in both time and money, and the order books were

A Kitson-Meyer articulated 2-6-6-2T locomotive for the FCAB railway that climbed to an altitude of 3,698 metres from the Chilean coast at Antofagasta. The line was originally 2ft 6in gauge but upgraded to metre gauge by the time this locomotive had been delivered in 1912.

showing fewer and fewer entries in the early thirties. In 1934, a receiver was appointed, and an attempt made to keep the company at work, but an order for an 0-8-0 tank engine for Jamaica in 1938 proved to be the last. Patterns and drawings were acquired by Robert Stephenson & Hawthorn and the business closed down.

Charles Todd was the Todd of Todd, Kitson & Laird and in 1838 he left that company to start his own works with a Mr. Shepherd – the Railway Foundry in Hunslet. Shepherd & Todd were to build both locomotives and rolling stock. Their first orders came in 1839 for two locomotives, followed by orders from the North Midland, the Manchester & Leeds and the Paris-Orleans Railways. The most interesting engines were built for the H&SR in 1840, where John Gray had just been appointed as locomotive superintendent. He had previously worked for the L&MR, and while there had developed the first expansion valve gear, which allowed for variable cut off and expansion of the stem in the cylinder. It was a somewhat ungainly gear, known as the 'horse leg motion' and difficult to operate, requiring a double lever to move the mechanism. It was first installed in the Cyclops locomotive for the L&MR, and was now to be used in the engines to be built for the H&SR. The other distinctive feature of the engines were the two domes, one above the firebox and the other in the more conventional position above the boiler.

Todd left the firm in 1844 and a year later E.B. Wilson joined the company but left the following year. In 1846 the company was taken over by James Fenton, an experienced Scottish engineer who had earlier been locomotive superintendent of first the Manchester & Leeds and then the Leeds & Thirsk Railway. The new concern was now known as Fenton Craven & Co. A large part of the output was of Stephenson long boiler type engines. This partnership was also short lived and in 1846 E.B. Wilson was back at the Leeds works taking over the whole company and retaining Fenton as works manager. The Railway Foundry was now home to yet another renamed company. E.B. Wilson & Co. It marked the beginning of a period of expansion that included the construction pf a new erection shop that now enabled them to increase output from ten a year to at least five times as many.

The new company received a number of orders and in 1846 their chief draughtsman, David Joy, was sent down to Brighton to make tracings for what was intended to be a set of ten 2-2-2 locomotives, designed by John Gray for the London, Brighton & South Coast Railway. But Gray was dismissed and his successor, Thomas Kirtley, was not happy with many aspects of the design, especially the Gray valve gear. Joy returned to Leeds, and he and James Fenton set to work adapting the original design. The first obvious change was to replace the Gray gear with the recently invented Stephenson. There were some admirable features in the original, including the use of a double frame. The inner frame held the cylinders and the 6ft diameter driving wheels and bearings: the outer frame held the 4ft diameter leading and trailing wheels. Gray had been one of the first to recognise that the common belief that engines needed a low centre of gravity was mistaken, but Kirtley still held to the old view. The result was a medium sized boiler, but working at what was for the time the high pressure of 120psi. Named *Jenny Lind* after the then famous soprano, the engine proved to steam well and be economical. There were initial problems with the strength of the frame but that was to be strengthened in later models. The engine was to prove a great success for the company, setting a new standard for passenger locomotives and altogether seventy were built, including twenty-four for the Midland. Later bigger versions, known as 'large Jennies' were later built.

The company introduced standardisation in their models in which the basic six-wheeled engines were available as 2-2-2, 2-4-0, 0-4-2 or 0-6-0. Very few were built as tank engines.

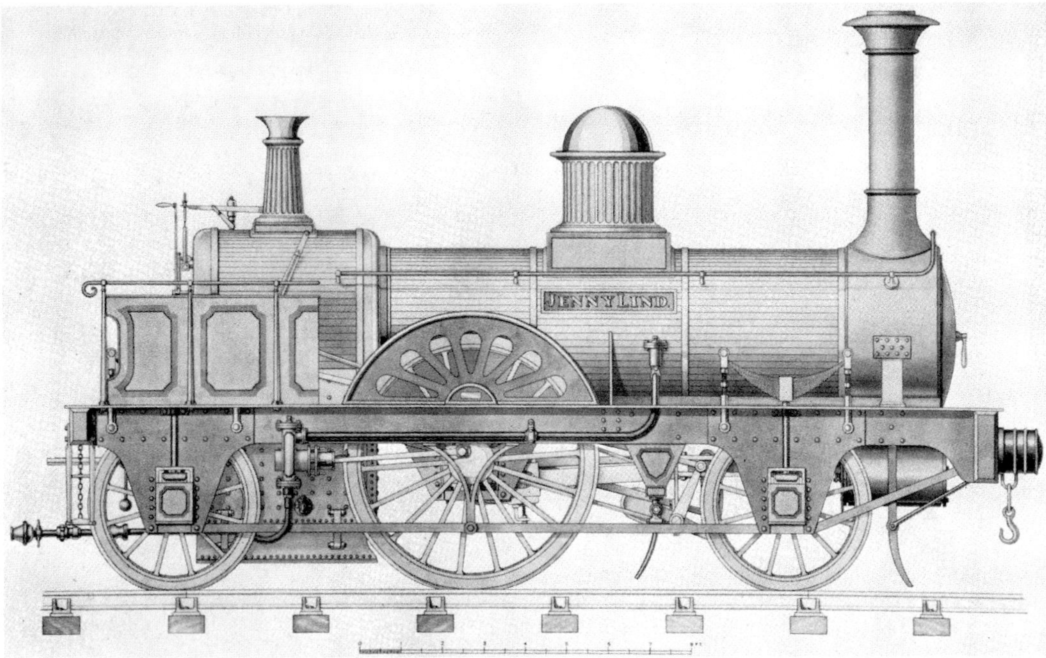

***Jenny Lind*, built for the London, Brighton & South Coast Railway in 1847 by E.B. Wilson.**

They could be supplied at affixed price if the customer was prepared to accept one of the standard models, otherwise changes cost extra. Over the years, 635 engines were built at the foundry. The company was forced into liquidation in 1858 and parts of the factory were taken over by our next company, Manning Wardle, in 1860.

Manning Wardle was first established in 1858 at the Boyne engineering works in Jack Lane. Alexander Campbell had been works manager at E.B. Wilson. When Wilson died, Campbell began looking for a partner to provide the finance to start up a new company and he was able to make a deal with a local vicar, Rev. C.W. Wardle. A new partner was added when John Manning joined the company. Not surprisingly, the company initially based their engines on the designs purchased from E.B. Wilson, but later developed a thriving business providing tank engines for railway contractors and industrial lines. The latter would include narrow gauge lines and, in fact, the first locomotive they built was for the 3ft 6in gauge line at the

Dunstan & Barlow iron works at Sheepbridge in Derbyshire that opened in 1857. Their next order in 1859 went to the opposite extreme with two 2-4-0 well tanks for the 5ft 6in gauge Royal Portuguese Railway and there were other orders for standard gauge tank engines the same year. 1860 saw the building of their only 2-2-2 passenger engines, when two were ordered by the New South Wales Government Railway.

The main work of the company over the next few years was to be the construction of 0-4-0 and 0-6-0 tank engines for constructors. They were all very basic, standard models, originally with just a simple weather board for the driver, which in later versions was curved to provide overhead cover. A distinctive feature was the tall, curved safety valve. They were so important to the company that of the 760 engines built by 1780, 609 of them were these tank engines. Because of standardisation, they were comparatively cheap – customers wanting variations had to pay extra and wait longer for delivery. Examples are to be found on preserved lines around the world. One of them, appropriately, survives on the line where it was first used by the contractor who built it. *Sharpthorn,* built in 1877 for the contractor Joseph Firbank, who worked on building the Lewes & East Grinstead Railway. Part of the route has been preserved as the Bluebell Line and they now own the engine.

Although primarily associated with workaday industrial engines, the company did become involved with the system designed by John Barraclough Fell for coping with steep gradients. Like a rack railway, it had a central rail, but instead of being a cog and pinion system, the plain rail was gripped on either side by separate drive wheels. The first use was during the construction of the tunnel under Mount Ceris but was dismantled when the tunnel was completed. The first line to use the method to overcome severe gradients was the Contagalo Railway in Brazil, which climbed from the coastal plain to a height of 1,100m, with gradients with a

The 0-6-0 saddle tank *Sharpthorn* built by Manning Wardle in 1877 on the Bluebell Railway.

steep section of 10km at 1 in 12. It was a narrow gauge line, probably 1m gauge. Manning Wardle supplied three 0-4-0 tank engines in 1873.

The Fell system was widely used, and we shall meet it again later, but Fell also designed what was known as a 'suspension railway' for use by the military. The narrow gauge track, that could be varied from 8in to 18in gauge was carried above a single row of pillars. The height of the pillars could be adjusted to suit the terrain, carrying the track anything from 3ft to 20ft above the ground. As well as conventional driving wheels, the engine was fitted with horizontal wheels to grip the outside of the track. Twenty miles of 18in gauge track were built by the Royal Engineers at Aldershot and the locomotive was built by Manning Wardle to Fell's design. Trials were held in 1872, with the engine and trucks, similarly fitted with horizontal gripping wheels, and were declared satisfactory. It was intended to use the system if campaign conditions needed a rail system that could be easily and rapidly assembled; it was never, it seems, used in wartime. The military connection was continued in 1882 when they supplied two 0-4-0STs for the War Department that were sent to the Sudan, where Gordon was leading the campaign against the Mahdi. They were supplied with armour plating and although armour plated trains had been used in earlier conflicts, including the American Civil War, they were conventional locomotives with the plating added later. The Manning Wardles are thought to be the first to be built with the plating included in the production process.

The company made important developments in the narrow gauge world, starting with *Lord Raglan* an 0-4-0 ST, built for the Royal Arsenal's 18in gauge line in 1871, the first of a series of similar engines. Although tank engines remained their main business, they did build some tender engines, starting with an 0-6-0 locomotive for the 2ft 6in gauge Pentewan

The Fell suspension railway locomotive *Ariel* built by Manning Wardle for Aldershot.

Railway that joined the china clay mines near St. Austell with the harbour of Charlestown. They were to build for a variety of narrow gauge lines around the world. At home, they proved successful on a number of lines, including the Vale of Rydal and the Lynton & Barnstaple.

Another area of interest that developed in the 1860s was steam tram engines. Th first was supplied to Brazil for a 4ft gauge tramway being built at Recife. It is claimed to be the first city in the world to run a street tramway with purpose-built steam locomotives. Rio de Janeiro had an earlier tramway but with conventional locomotives. Manning Wardle provided two 0-4-0ST engines in 1866 in which the exhaust steam was condensed in the saddle tank. The engine was boxed in. Later, the line was extended to Olinda and again Manning Wardle provided the engines. In spite of being pioneers in designing tram engines, this was never an important part of their business.

Another new development was the construction of crane engines, the first of which went to Kirkstall Forge in Leeds in 1875. I would like to think that it was received by the works foreman at the time, my great-great grandfather. Crane tanks were also exported over the years, but in the early years of the twentieth century the company concentrated on their tank engine business with engines being sent to Australia, New Zealand, Europe, India and South America. Like other manufacturers, during 1914-18 production was limited in Britain to supplying essential industries such as coal and steel, though overseas orders were still coming in. They did, however, briefly abandon steam locomotives, producing ten petrol engines locomotives, with the 180hp engines supplied by Thornycroft. They were armour plated and were originally intended for use with heavy artillery on railed tracks. They were not up to the task and were used merely for shunting.

The 1920s were difficult times for all locomotive manufacturers, and Manning Wardle had done little to change the way they worked since they started in the middle of the nineteenth century. In 1927 they went into voluntary liquidation. Over the years, 2,004 locomotives had left the Leeds factory. They were never glamorous manufacturers – none of their engines was designed for breaking speed records or hauling luxury trains. They, however, had few rivals when it came to producing reliable engines to serve a busy, industrial world.

A new company was set up in Leeds in 1860, taking over part of the old E.B. Wilson Railway Foundry site. The two founding members were both former employees, William Shillito Hudswell, former chief draughtsman, and works manager John Clarke. Originally known as Hudswell & Clarke, it was later abbreviated to just Hudswell Clarke. The finance for building a new works on the site was supplied by an eminent local surgeon, William Clayton. Their very first construction was not a locomotive, but a stationary steam engine, and over the years they were to undertake other engineering work, including a lucrative sideline in manufacturing pulley systems for mills and the famous 'Tom Pudding' compartment boats for use on the Aire & Calder Canal. Locomotive construction, however, was soon to dominate the business. The first two locomotives of 1861 were 0-6-0 saddle tanks for a new line under construction from the Mountain Colliery in Flint to Connah's Quay on the River Dee. They were the first of many four and six-coupled tank engines that were to be built over the years. Unlike Manning Wardle, however, they did not rely on their own standard designs, but advertised that they were ready to take on any orders.

One of the biggest orders came from the Manchester Ship Canal when construction began in 1887. The contractors' engines were specially designed for the job. They were 0-6-0 side tank engines in which the centre wheels were flangeless to help with negotiating many tight curves on the track. Altogether, 173 locomotives were in use, 24 of which were supplied by Hudswell Clarke. With construction completed, many went into use on the Ship Canal's own railway system and the company continued to supply locomotives, later changing from steam to diesel engines. Ten similar tank engines were supplied to the Port of London Authority.

An important contract came from another local Company. Robert Hudswell was established at Gilderstone near Leeds in 1865 and began manufacturing rails and rolling stock, but not locomotives. They entered into an agreement with Hudswell Clarke to supply sixteen standard design engines that would be sold by Hudswell. During the First World War, Robert Hudswell supplied light rails to the War Office, intended for use as temporary lines that could be laid anywhere they were needed. At the same time, they also supplied 0-6-0WT engines, suitable for use with the light rails. Some of the largest tank engines Hudswell Clarke built for narrow gauge lines went to Ireland. In 1904 a 2-6-0T was bought by the 3ft gauge roadside Castleberg & Victoria Bridgeway tramway in County Tyrone. It was followed by a 0-4-4T that proved easier to handle on the somewhat twisty track. Both were still in use when the line closed in 1933. Ireland was also the home to the two biggest engines ever to leave the works, 4-8-4Ts for the 5ft 6in gauge Londonderry & Lough Swilly Railway.

Although tank engines remained important to the company, they did not entirely monopolise output. In the 1840s, the North Staffordshire Railway had been supplied by a number of Jones and Potts 2-4-0s and Robert Stephenson 0-6-0s which the company rebuilt, some as tank engines. In 1907, they built two steam railcars, with bodywork by Cravens, for the Rhymney Railway. The engine section was basically an adaptation of an 0-4-0 tank, which was later separated from the passenger compartments and refigured as a 0-6-0. The depression years of the 1930s saw a drop in orders. During the Second World War, however, they were kept busy and in 1943 they received their biggest order for fifty 'Austerity' 0-6-0ST locomotives. Work on

Hudswell Clarke 0-6-0 tank engine of 1906 at the Welsh Industrial Museum, Cardiff.

steam locomotives continued after the war. In 1950 they built four 2-6-2 tender locomotives for the 2ft 6in gauge Dehri Rotas Light Railway in India. Perhaps the oddest locomotive they built was for the Esholt sewage works near Leeds. Although apparently a conventional 0-6-0 saddle tank, it was specially designed to be fuelled by wool grease, a by-product of the treatment of effluent from local mills. Their very last steam locomotive was built in 1961, rather appropriately, a standard 0-4-0ST for the National Coal Board – so their last steam engine, like their first, was for a colliery.

Unlike the other Leeds firms we have looked at so far, Hudswell Clarke recognised that they needed to develop other locomotives, not just steam, as a great many ex war

Hudswell Clake steam rail car No.1 of 1907 for the Rhymney Railway.

department engines were available at reasonable prices after 1918. They had received a German Deutz petrol engine, and they decided to start developing their own versions. The first given the prefix P for petrol, P251, was built in 1925 and sold to Leeds Corporation for a major road-building project that involved a vast amount of earthworks. This was followed by fifteen narrow gauge petrol engines. They also built a petrol railcar, for which the bodywork was supplied by a Leeds bus manufacturer, Charles H. Roe. It was designed for the military Spurn Point Railway, built to reach the fort at the end of the long spit of land. One curious feature of the line was that locals were allowed to use it with special carts that quite literally sailed along.

It soon became clear that diesel was a far more appropriate fuel for locomotives than petrol. Their first diesel, D557, was a direct drive engine built for the Junin Railway in Chile in 1930 and was at the time the most powerful of its kind in the world. The following year saw a very different order. Seaside holidays by rail were becoming increasingly popular, and part of the excitement came from traveling to the resort behind a powerful express locomotive. The North Bay amusement park in Scarborough built a miniature railway almost a mile long and ordered two diesel engines from Hudswell Clarke, but they were designed to look like the famous LNER A3 Pacific steam locomotives. The first two were named *Neptune* and *Triton* and were later joined by *Poseidon*. They are still at work, offering a round trip of two miles. Other orders for diesel-powered, imitation steam locomotives soon came from other resorts, including Blackpool and the new Butlin's Holiday Camp at Clacton. These were not toys but gave the company an opportunity to experiment with new transmission technology, especially hydraulic transmission instead of direct drive. *Neptune* is the oldest surviving example of this form of transmission in the world.

The Second World War saw the company continuing to manufacture locomotives but, like many other locomotive builders, also had to take on other work, including the manufacture of missile parts. This work continued after the war, when they become involved in providing material for the atomic bomb tests. They were to continue with non-railway projects, even when the demand for locomotives returned. In 1958, the company built an experimental 0-6-0 diesel shunter named *Enterprise* that was given trials at various locations, including collieries and Skelton Grande Power Station. The diesel engine was fitted with a Brown Boveri supercharger and transmission was based on the Hi-Dyne principal, where the torque decreased with increased speed – meaning that most power was available for low speed work, such as shunting. It was not entirely successful, but it did lead to an important order from Sierra Leone for a 2ft 6in gauge railway. The company supplied eight 0-8-0 and twenty-four 2-8-2 locomotives, based on the *Enterprise* prototype.

A profitable market for the company was the newly nationalised coal industry, where a modernisation programme

The miniature railway diesel locomotive *Poseidon*, disguised to look like an LNER A3, at Scarborough.

Hudswell Clarke diesel built in 1966 for the Mersey Docks and Harbour Board, now preserved at the Middleton Railway.

was under way. They supplied large numbers of narrow gauge diesels for use underground. They worked in conjunction with Hugh, Wood & Co, who supplied mining equipment and the engine were known as Huwood Hudswells. By the 1960s, however, there was a lack of orders for locomotives, and the company turned increasingly to civil engineering projects, and much of the locomotive business was taken over by our next locomotive company, Hunslet, though the name Hudswell Clarke remained in use for some time. In 1958, the entire company was taken over by the Industrial & Commercial

Finance Corporation. Their days of locomotive construction were over.

The Hunslet Engine Company was founded in 1864 by John Towlerton Leather, a civil engineer whose family also had investments in local industries, including the Waterloo colliery near Leeds, opened in 1815 and taking its name from the famous battle of that year. Leather took over another part of the old Railway Foundry site, which was already home to several of the locomotive builders already discussed. There was, it seems, still room for another builder in that area of Leeds. The first engine was, inevitably it seems for Leeds manufacturers, a 0-6-0 saddle tank for the famous railway contractor, Thomas Brassey who was at work on building the Midland Railway, on which Leather himself had also been a contractor. It would have been normal practice for the business to be taken over eventually by John Leather's son, Arthur, but for some reason that did not work out. James Campbell, son of Alexander Campbell of Manning Wardle, was brought in as manager. After a sluggish start, Campbell became owner of the company, and business began to show a notable improvement. Like the other Leeds companies, the mainstay of the business was in four- and six-coupled tank engines.

There were some variations in the early years. In 1871 they built a vertical boiler 2-2-0 well tank inspection car for the Oudh & Rohikund Railway in northern India. The basic engine was shipped out and the seating and superstructure were completed on arrival. Another one-off was a condensing engine of a type designed by Léon Francq for the Novelle-Orleans à Carrollton tramway. The condensing system used 950 one-inch tubes but was not a great success. The most remarkable locomotives supplied in these early days have to be the ones designed for the Listowel & Balybunion monorail system. It was devised by the French engineer Charles Latigue. The track was not strictly a monorail as, apart from the main load bearing rail, there were rails on either side at a lower level. The locomotive overhung the central rail on both sides, with wheels on all three rails, giving the engines an odd 0-3-0-wheel arrangement. The line was opened in 1888 and a section has recently been restored.

An important line for the company began in 1870 when they supplied a prototype 0-4-0 saddle tank *Dinorwic* to the famous slate quarry of the same name. The track was laid to an apparently arbitrary 1ft 10¾in gauge. More orders followed over the next few years with various improvements, culminating in the Alice Class of 1886 – one obvious difference between Dinorwic and the later engines was the provision of a covered cab for the footplate crew. They were to continue to supply quarry engines for many years, several of which are still in service on preserved lines.

Although four-coupled tank engines remained a vital part of the company's business throughout the steam age, they did make larger versions of their quarry engines for several narrow gauge lines in Wales. North Wales Narrow Gauge

Hunslet 0-3-0 locomotive No. 1 on the Listowel & Balybunion monorail system c.1890.

Railways was a company formed in 1872 to build a network of lines in the Snowdonia region and Hunslet supplied them with a number of engines, starting with the 0-6-4 saddle tank, *Beddgelert* in 1878 and ending with a the 0-6-4T single Fairlie in 1908. One of these engines, the 2-6-2T *Russell,* still runs on part of the old network, now known as the Welsh Highland Railway, linking Caernarfon to Porthmadog. The 3ft gauge Tralee & Dingle Light Railway ordered contractors' engines in 1889. These were conventional 2-6-0 tanks, except that, as they were constantly running backward and forwards along the line, they were fitted with cabs at both ends. When the line was opened in 1891, the cabs were removed. Hunslet were to go on to provide more engines for the line, including larger 2-6-2 tanks. Several variations on the 2-6-2 tank engine theme appeared over the years, including three built for the 2ft 6in gauge Sierra Leone Government Railway in 1898. These proved highly successful and thirty-two of the class were built over the next half century. Among the more curious engines produced and sent to Africa were built for the 2ft 6in Lagos Steam Tramway in 1901, a single track narrow gauge line. They were articulated locomotives, the first half of which was a conventional outside cylinder 0-4-0 tank, but with a shortened back fitted with a ball joint to which was attached what looked like a square shed on a 4-wheel bogie. This contained the coal bunker and water tank. Like most tram engines, the wheels and motion were hidden behind plated sides.

In 1902, the decision was taken to change from a privately owned firm to a public company, becoming Hunslet Engine Co. Ltd. When James Campbell died in 1905, three of his sons took active roles, with Alexander as chairman, Robert works manager and Will as secretary. The arrangement did not prove a great success, and in 1912 Edgar Alcock, who had been assistant works manager for Beyer Peacock, took over from Robert Campbell. He began reorganising work and was at the start of a transition that involved building

4-6-4 tank engine of 1913 on the 2ft 6in gauge Kendi Valley line, Sri Lanka c.1920.

ever bigger engines. In 1913 they supplied the first of a series of 2-8-4 tank engines to the 2ft gauge Antofagasta & Bolivia Railway. The line was later relaid as a 1m gauge line, and the company provided more 2-8-2T engines in the 1920s.The outbreak of war in 1914 saw many major changes. Like many other companies, they had to diversify and began working on munitions, which brought women onto the factory floor for the first time in the company's history. In 1916, they began building 4-6-0 tanks for the War Office. Like other providers of engines for use in Europe, they had to meet the strict conditions laid down by the War Department, to allow them to be used on the temporary narrow-gauge tracks. Weight had to be limited to 3½tons and they had to be able to cope with curves of 20m radius. Altogether they produced 155 of these engines between 1916 and 1919.

After the war, the demand for larger engines grew and the erection shop was extended and the works modernised. Overseas orders became increasingly important, including twenty-six 1m gauge superheated 4-6-0s for India. The biggest engines were 0-8-0 standard gauge tank engines for marshalling trains on the Nanking ferry in China. Built in 1933, they weighed in at 85 tons and they were the most powerful tank engines in the world at that time. There were also orders nearer home, including one for ninety London Midland & Scottish Class 3F, 0-6-0 tanks, designed by Fowler and first introduced in 1924. This was a highly successful class of engine, with 422 being built in all.

In 1932, the company produced engine 1697, their first lightweight, 21hp diesel shunter. This was a time when many companies had collapsed for lack of orders, among them Kerr Surat, who had begun designing diesels at their works in Stoke-on-Trent in the 1920s. Hunslet had acquired their designs and good will and used this to advantage in producing their own design. It was shown at the British Industries Fair and was given trials at the local LMS goods yard.

They continued with their main business of building tank engines until the start of the Second World War. Like other companies they had to diversify, producing a variety of non-locomotive items from aircraft parts to anti-tank guns. Their main contribution was the 'Austerity' locomotive. When the government were looking for a standard locomotive, they considered a number of options, including the LMS standard 3F Class, designed by Henry Fowler and introduced in 1924, some of which were built in the 1930s by Hunslet, Eventually, however, it was decided to go with Hunslet's own 0-6-0 saddle tanks, and over the years, 487 of these industrial workhorses were built, 217 at Hunslet. After the war, Hunslet continued

A National Coal Board Austerity tank engine at Bickershaw Colliery in 1983.

to provide these engines to the National Coal Board, and the last of them, No. 3890, went to Cadeby colliery in 1964. It was not the last steam locomotive to leave the works. They did, however, receive orders though their South African subsidiary to build eight articulated Beyer-Garretts for South African Railways in the 1960s. Their final order came as late as 1971, for a 0-4-2 saddle tank, based on the 'Brazil' series, originally produced by Kerr Stuart. It was sent to a sugar mill at Pati in Java, and was named *Tangkil,* after the mill's name. The engine has since been returned to Britain.

Although it marked the end of construction for steam locomotives, it did not stop the company's involvement. They undertook repairs and restoration work on a number of locomotives for the newly developing steam preservation movement, starting with work on a former Corris Railway Kerr Stuart 0-4-2 ST locomotive built in 1921 for the pioneering Talyllyn Railway. It was restored to working order in 1952 and named *Edward Thomas.* They worked on a number of prestige locomotives over the years, including *Flying Scotsman* and the Jubilee Class 4-6-0 *Bahamas*.

In the post war years, the company increasingly turned to diesel manufacture. They soon developed engines far more powerful than their 1932 prototype. Their 0-6-0 shunters, mostly fitted with 204hp Gardner engines, were to have the same significance in the industrial world as the 0-6-0STs had in the steam age. Even bigger 1124hp Bo-Bo engines were introduced in the 1970s. Diesels for use in mines were an important part of the business, and they became involved in providing material for the Bercorit system, a form of monorail, in that the train was carried on a single rail, but rails laid to either side at ground level were gripped by extra wheels to provide stability. In Ireland, a great deal of electricity was provided from power stations using peat as a fuel instead of coal, but still required locomotives for transport. Bord na Móna, the Irish company that operated the system, wanted a standard set of engines and they opted for the Hunslet Waggonmasters, 0-4-0 diesel hydraulics, powered by Ford 80hp engines.

In 1984, they took over the neighbouring firm of Greenwood & Batley. They were a general engineering company, established in 1856 with a wide range of products and began building battery-powered electric locomotives in 1927, under the trade name Greenbat. Among their orders inherited by Hunslet was one for their London Mail Train locomotives. This was for a narrow gauge underground line, linking major sorting offices in the capital. These were electrically operated, like the rest of the London underground system, but Hunslet did not immediately pursue further contracts for electric locomotives.

The miners' strike of 1984-5 had been called in an attempt to prevent pit closures, but when it failed the Thatcher government began a huge programme of pit closures, which not only devastated mining communities across Britain, but in effect killed off the home market for colliery engines and this hit the Hunslet company very hard. In 1987, they were taken over by Telfos Holdings. They were able shortly afterwards to provide engines for the most important engineering project of the age – the Channel Tunnel. Work began in 1988. The following year, they received an order for electric locomotives for the Tyne & Wear Metro.

In 1991, there was another takeover, this time by the Austrian firm Jenbacher, founded in 1959, which had specialised in producing gas and diesel engines and also had begun manufacturing railcars. They invested heavily in Leeds, building a new erection shop, and their main orders were for the British Rail Class 323 multiple units. A new company – Hunslet Transportation Projects – had been set up in Birmingham. In 1990 they began the design work on the three-car electric trains, intended for suburban lines in the Birmingham and Manchester area, but the Leeds works did the actual construction and fitting out. Altogether, forty-three units were built. A potential order for what would have been Class 157 Sprinter units for Strathclyde disappeared with the privatisation of the railway system, which meant funding for development disappeared. The Hunslet works closed in 1995, ending nearly two centuries of locomotive construction in Leeds.

Thomas Green & Son began by manufacturing agricultural machinery in 1848 and only began making locomotives in 1884, when they saw an opening in the market for steam tram engines. Many were based on the design of William Wilkinson (p.180), geared engines with vertical boilers. They were nearly all of the enclosed type used on most tramways, but they also built 2-4-2s for the Dublin & Bressington

A Hunslet diesel-mechanical, one of a class built between 1958 and 1961, seen here at Goole in 1961.

Tramway, which had a cab at each end, with the fireman remaining at just the one end, and the driver using each cab according to the direction the train was travelling. In all, they built some 200 tram engines. In 1898, they began building conventional industrial locomotives, including three 2-6-2Ts for the 3ft gauge West Clare Railway in Ireland. The rest of the thirty-eight locomotives bult by 1920 were six-wheeled tanks.

Chapter Five

Hawthorn

Robert Hawthorn began manufacturing marine and stationary steam engines at the Forth Bank Works in Newcastle-upon-Tyne in 1817. In 1820 he was joined by his brother William, and the company became R&W Hawthorn. They are believed to have gone, like many other engineers, to Rainhill for the locomotive trials and recognised that they were seeing the beginning of a new railway age, which would offer opportunities. They were not, in fact, the first in the family to take an interest in railways. Their father, also Robert Hawthorn, had gone to Wylam in 1811 to see the test carriage being put through its paces. This interesting device, was a four-wheeled platform, in which the wheels were turned through gears, operated by levers worked by two men. When the system proved satisfactory, work went ahead on developing a steam locomotive. There is some dispute over the first locomotive. James W. Lowe in *British Steam Locomotive Builders* (2014) is one of several who claim that it was an engine called *Modling*, built in 1831 for the Vienna-Gloggnitz line, but this is unlikely as the line was not opened until 1841. Other authorities claim a much more likely venue for the first engine was for the S&DR, and add that *Modling* was delivered in 1841.

In 1831, Timothy Hackworth produced two versions of 0-6-0 locomotives, the Wilberforce and Majestic classes. One of the curious features of both classes was the positioning of the vertical cylinders in front of the smoke box on an extended frame. Altogether there were six of each class built between 1831 and 1832, half by Hawthorn and half by Robert Stephenson. One reason that Hawthorn may have got the contract was that they had already supplied a stationary engine for working the Brusselton incline on the S&DR. Later engines built for the line were the 0-4-0 *Swift* with vertical cylinders and an inside cylinder 2-2-0, *Sunbeam*. Both were designed and constructed by Hawthorn in 1837. The engines had Hawthorn's own design of valve gear, using a complex arrangement of swivelling blocks and rocking arms that can be seen in the illustration below.

In 1838, they built two locomotives designed by Thomas Elliot Harrison, better known as a civil engineer than as a mechanical. They were specifically built to satisfy the stringent conditions initially laid down by Brunel for the GWR. In order to ensure a good supply of steam while keeping the weight of the locomotive down, the engines

Hawthorn locomotive
Swift built for the Stockton & Darlington in 1837, featuring Hawthorn's own complex valve gear.

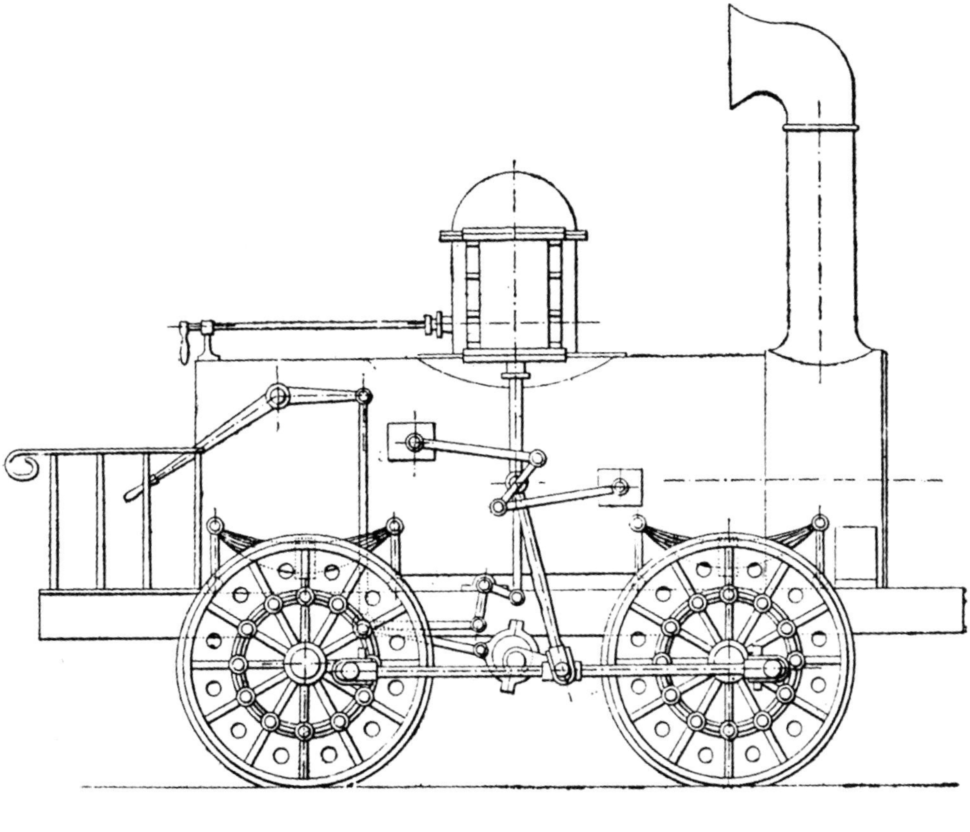

had the boilers placed on one carriage and the cylinders and driving gear on another, the two being joined by flexible tubing. The drive wheels on *Thunderer* were 6ft diameter, but they were operated through gears with a 3:1 ratio, providing the equivalent of a 18ft wheel. The other engine, *Hurricane,* had no gearing but was fitted with 10ft drive wheels. Although *Thunderer* was said to have achieved a speed of 60mph, neither engine was a success, suffering endless breakdowns. Within a year of being delivered, both were withdrawn, but they are historically interesting as a first attempt to create articulated locomotives.

The company developed a thriving export business, supplying locomotives for lines in Europe, South Africa, South America, India and Australia. Among the more interesting products were four 4-2-0 Cramptons for the Zealand Railway in Denmark, built in 1854. They were successful, but the same cannot be said for a set of six 4-4-0 saddle tank Cramptons supplied to the East Kent Railway in 1857. They gave endless troubles, were constantly breaking down and were soon taken out of service. The fault was with the basic design, not the manufacture, and in 1860 they were rebuilt as 0-4-0Ts, which proved satisfactory.

Like many other companies, they had standard designs for four- and six-coupled industrial tank engines available. They also supplied fireless and crane locomotives. In 1870 they built the St Peter's works, next to Robert Stephenson & Co.'s Forth Street works, mainly for marine engineering projects. The shipbuilding interest was expanded even further, when they acquired A. Leslie & Co. of Hebburn on the south bank of the Tyne, becoming Hawthorn Leslie & Co.

In 1893, they built a 4-2-2-0 locomotive, *James Toleman,* designed by the British engineer William Charles Winby. It had four cylinders for the two sets of drive wheels. It was sent to the Columbia Exhibition in Chicago, after which it was sent to work on the Chicago, Milwaukee & St. Paul Railroad.

Hawthorn Leslie 0-6-0T on the metre gauge Transandian Railway that ran from Valparaiso, Chile to Mendoza, Argentina, photographed in 1891 by Leo Wherli.

There were no immediate orders for other engines with this wheel arrangement, though some were later built for the London & South Western Railway (L&SWR). In general, however, more conventional four-coupled engines proved more effective, and no more of this configuration were ever built. Among the other unusual engines built at the turn of the century was an 0-8-0T for the Kent & East Sussex Railway and there does not seem to have been any other locomotive of this wheel arrangement ever supplied to a light railway – which is hardly surprising. It soon proved its unsuitability and was sold on to the Southern Railway. A steam railcar for the Port Talbot Railway & Docks Co. in 1907 was the largest of the kind ever built. It was six-coupled and had an overall length of 76ft. The carriage bodywork was by Hurst, Nelson. Both carriage compartment and locomotive section were faced with metal to give a uniform appearance. It remained in use on the line until 1915, after which it was sent to the Millwall Extension Railway and was finally withdrawn in 1926.

The early twentieth century saw the company extending their Forth Street works onto part of the site once occupied by Robert Stephenson & Co. In the years before the First World War, they produced a number of large tank engines. One of the more curious incidents involved a design by Frederick George Smith, Locomotive Superintendent at the Highland Railway works. This was for six 4-6-0 tanks, with 8ft drive wheels. When they were delivered, the Chief Engineer rejected them, on the grounds that they were too heavy for

South Indian Railways 2-6-4T, works number 4117.

the line. Smith resigned, and the engines were taken by the Caledonian. Among the other large steam engines were a number of 0-6-2 tanks for the Shropshire & Montgomery and the Taff Vale railways.

They also produced an interesting range of fireless locomotives, specially designed for use on sites, such as gunpowder factories, where the risk of explosions was high. The locomotives themselves had no fireboxes or conventional boilers but were fitted with steam reservoirs. Steam was raised in a separate boiler bouse, well away from the danger area. Hot water and high-pressure steam were forced into the reservoir, where the heat evaporated the water to produce more steam, but at a lower pressure. The engine could be worked over short distances, but when pressure dropped below a certain point, it had to return to be recharged with steam.

The company continued working into the 1930s, expanding their business by building a number of 0-6-0 diesel shunters

Crane locomotive of 1909, ordered by Hawthorn's French agent, Henning.

that would be the basis for the British Rail O8 class. Working with English Electric, they also began constructing electric locomotives, offering a choice of battery operated or powered by a diesel generator. They had the advantage that they could be used without the expense of infrastructure needed for electrifying the actual line. In 1937, the locomotive department was taken over and became R. Stephenson & Hawthorn Ltd. The outbreak of war in 1939 brought a major change, but the company was able to continue manufacturing locomotives, mainly for the Ministry of Supply, that included an order for sixty 0-6-0ST Austerity Class engines, that were built between 1943 and 1945. In 1944, the Vulcan Foundry took a major share in the company. It had been started back in 1930

Diesel 0-4-0 built by Robert Stephenson & Hawthorn in 1954 and worked at the Blue Boar Wharf, Rochester.

by Robert Stephenson and Charles Tayleur, so it was quite fitting that the two companies with which Robert had been intimately concerned were now united. Foreign orders still dominated, though the company also manufactured L1 and 9400 Class locomotives for the newly formed nationalised company, British Rail.

The last conventional steam locomotive, an 0-6-0 tank, was built in 1959 and the very last, built the following year, was a fireless locomotive. In the post war years, however, the company continued constructing diesel and electric locomotives. The joint company's first diesel was built in 1937 with a direct reversing engine – one without a reversing gear, but where the Crossley 2-stroke engine could be reversed. In the post war years, they built Classes O4, 20, 37 and 40 for British rail, as well as supplying engines to Australia and New Zealand. Among the electric locomotives built for the overseas market were the handsome EW Class, built for the New Zealand Railway and the first in that country with a Bo-Bo-Bo wheel arrangement. Forth Street finally closed in 1960 and the Darlington works were taken over by English Electric in 1962 for the manufacture of diesel and electric locomotives. It was the end of an era that had seen wo famous companies at the forefront of locomotive development.

Chapter Six

North British and its Constituent Companies

The story begins with Richard Roberts, a remarkably inventive mechanical engineer who established a business in Manchester in 1816, having previously worked for the great engineer Henry Maudsley. He soon began manufacturing a range of machine tools, and later turned to textile machinery, in which his most notable contribution was the self-acting mule, used for spinning. In 1822, he went into partnership with an iron merchant, Thomas Sharp. In 1828 they opened

Hibernia built by Sharp Roberts for the Dublin & Kingstown Railway in 1834.

LOCOMOTIVE ENGINE—DUBLIN AND KINSTOWN RAILWAY.

the Atlas Works in Great Bridgewater Street, Manchester. It was here that they began manufacturing locomotives. It is somewhat ironic that the engines were invariably known as Sharps or Sharpies, although the initial engineering design work was all down to Roberts.

The company's first locomotive was the *Experiment*, built for the L&MR in 1833. It is a strangely old-fashioned looking engine for the time, with its vertical cylinders connected to the drive wheels by a complex arrangement from the cross head, via connecting rods and a bell crank. There were no eccentrics, and the valve gear was operated by means of a long connecting rod from the bell crank to the footplate. The system can be seen in the drawing of an almost identical locomotive *Hibernia*, built for the Dublin & Kingstown Railway in 1834. The bell crank is labelled N in the drawing. Neither locomotive was especially successful, largely because of steam leakages from the cylinders and mechanical problems

Sharp Roberts
Eagle built for the Great Western in 1838, drawn by E.T. Lane in 1840.

with the complex gear mechanism. Vertical cylinders and bell cranks were never to be used again, and later engines looked a good deal more conventional.

The next generation of engines were 2-2-2s, with what was to become a regular feature of Sharp engine, a combined tall dome and safety valve set close to the chimney, with a second safety valve above the firebox. The engines had outside frames and separate inside frames to carry the bearings. The initial order was for ten engines for the Grand Junction Railway in 1837, Literally hundreds more were built to this basic design over the next twenty years. The engines were exported to a variety of European countries, and a few variations of other six-wheel engines were produced, including tank engines, but the singles remained the dominant style. The changes may have been partly due to the arrival of a new man at the company in 1834, Charles Beyer. Roberts was happy to pass over much of the design work to Beyer, while he concentrated on other inventions – his turret clock won a prize at the Great Exhibition of 1851. We shall be meeting Beyer again shortly. In 1843, Roberts left the firm, which was renamed Sharp Brothers. In 1852 there was a further change, when John Sharp retired and was replaced by Charles Patrick Stewart, who had been born in Dublin in 1823, and the company became, Sharp, Stewart, later becoming a limited company.

One important development for the company was the acquisition of the sole rights to manufacture the Giffard injector. This had been invented by Henry Giffard in the 1850s and patented in France in 1858. To refill the boiler against the internal pressure, cold water is forced in by mixing water with steam in a combining cone and the steam is partially condensed and excess steam pressure forces the mixed jet into the delivery cone from which it can be fed as a high-speed jet to the boiler. The system is far more efficient than the mechanical pumping system previously in use.

Like other British companies, Sharp Stewart found a ready market for their locomotives in India. Their first were for the Great India Peninsula Railway, for which they supplied their first engines with more than six wheels. These were 4-6-0 saddle tanks for use in the two steep slopes, the Bhore and Thul Ghatts that were part of the system that zig-zagged up the cliffs that separated the central Indian plateau from the coastal plain. Their next Indian order was for the Oudh & Rohilkhand Railway, for which they supplied both 0-8-0 and 0-6-0 locomotives between 1865 and 1870. One of the 0-6-0s, No. B-26, is now preserved in the National Railway Museum in Delhi. It was originally used for mixed traffic between Lucknow and Kanpur and remained in service right through to 1921.

The most famous line for which Sharp Stewart provided locomotives was the narrow-gauge Darjeeling Himalayan, with its steep climbs eased by a series of loops and zigzags. The first locomotives to arrive were the 1 Class of 1880, but the specifications given to the manufacturers had underestimated the steepness of the gradients, and the engines struggled to cope. These were followed two years later by the more powerful A Class, fitted with a well tank between the frames, a larger boiler produced more steam, and in time a saddle tank was added. This arrangement of well and saddle tank was continued with the still more powerful B Class, the first being delivered in 1889. Fourteen are still to be found on the line. Production continued after Sharp Stewart became part of the North British Company.

The most unusual engines built by the company were for the Lisbon steam tramway. The story begins in France where J. Larmanjat designed a monorail tramway system. This was first used on a French tramway that opened in 1868, in which the locomotive had a 1-2-1 wheel arrangement, the leading and trailing wheels running on the rail, the drive wheels on the road to either side. It was not entirely successful and required a helmsman to manoeuvre it round bends. However, an English company was set up to build a tramway for Lisbon. The engines were designed by F.H. Trevithick, grandson of the famous locomotive pioneer. The system was the same as for the Paris tramway and first given a trial over short track set up at Buckhurst Hill in Epping Forest. The engines were saddle tanks but improved on the French original by having two sets of leading and trailing wheels running on the monorail, giving an unusual 1-1-2-1-1 arrangement. Sharp Stewart provided all the engines for use with the system.

By the 1880s, the Manchester works were at full capacity, and locomotive construction was still only part of the business. There was no room for expansion, so they began looking for new premises. Their choice was the works established in 1884 by Walter Nielson for the Clyde Locomotive Company (see p. 104). By 1888, when Sharp Stewart took them over, there were a few orders on the books, which were completed by Sharp Stewart, who set about reorganising the works and renaming it the 'Atlas Works'. They were soon to take on the major part of the company's locomotive business.

Overseas orders continued to form a vital part of the company's business. Among their customers was the 5ft 6in gauge Buenos Aires & Ensenada Port Railway for whom they

The trail of the Sharp No. 1a at Buckhurst Hill, Epping Forest before being sent to the Lisbon Steam Tramway.

TRIAL OF THE LISBON STEAM TRAMWAY CARRIAGE, AT BUCKHURST HILL

A Furness Railway 'Seagull' Class by Sharp Stewart, c.1900.

built their first 4-6-0s in 1884. The first British locomotives with this wheel arrangement, and at the time the most powerful engines in the country, were the 'Jones Goods' of 1894, designed for heavy freight on the Highland Railway by David Jones. Fourteen were built and one is now preserved at the Riverside Museum, Glasgow. Over the next decade, a number of imposingly large engines were built, including twelve 4-8-0 tanks and thirteen 4-8-0 tender locomotives for the 3ft 6in gauge Cape Government Railway and 0-6-0 tanks for the Imperial Japanese Railways, also constructed to a 3ft 6in gauge. Nearer home, one of their regular customers was the Barry Railway, with Sharp Stewart contributing a large number of tank engines of various configuration, including the B-Class 0-6-2 tanks and 0-6-2s originally intended for Norway. In 1903, the Atlas Works became home to North British following the amalgamation with Dübs and Neilson Reid & Co.

Neilson Reid was a later version of the company that began as Kerr, Neilson and Mitchell around 1836, but Kerr soon left and by 1848 it had become Nielson and Mitchell. Walter Neilson was the son of James Neilson, inventor of

South African Railway Class 8A, 4-8-0 built by Sharp Stewart in 1902, seen here at Breyton, Transvaal in 1961.

the hot blast furnace. Born in Glasgow, his initial training was at the Oakworth Foundry, after which he was employed at the Caledonian Railway's St. Rollox Works in Glasgow. James Mitchell appears to have been mainly concerned with the financial side of the business. They established works at Hyde Park Street in Glasgow in 1837, where they began manufacturing stationary and marine engines, work that continued right through to 1855. Their first locomotives were for the Glasgow & Garnkirk Railway which was opened in 1831, mainly to carry coal from the Monkland coalfield to Glasgow. It was originally horse drawn and was built to a 4ft 6in gauge. These were 0-4-0 engines and were followed by other modest locomotives for local lines, including a pair of 2-2-2 well tanks for the Edinburgh and Glasgow. *Wee*

Scotland and *Little England*. Some notable names appeared on the employment list in those early years. Patrick Stirling had earlier been employed at the Vulcan Foundry when he was taken on as works foreman in the 1840s and was later to become famous for the elegant Stirling Singles. Henry Dübs, who we shall be meting again shortly, was born in Germany and originally named Heinrich Dübs, but changed his name after emigrating to Britain and was appointed works manager in 1858, after spending time at Vulcan and Beyer Peacock.

The company were soon busy with orders from around the world, especially for India and later South Africa as well as maintaining a healthy order book for British customers. Their success meant that they were finding conditions increasingly cramped at the original site, so work began on developing a major new works in 1861 in Springburn that became the Hyde Park Works. A description of the works from 1888, when all their business had been transferred to the new site, tells of a progressive, well-organised factory and what the change meant to production. In 1865, with 1,000 men employed, they were turning out 82 engines and tenders a year but by 1885 they were employing 2,500 and producing 206 engines and tenders. Everything was arranged in a very logical manner. The first departments nearest the entrance yard were the pattern shop, where patterns were prepared for casting in the adjoining iron and brass foundries and there was also a template shop, where the templates for standard units were stored. The next range of buildings contained the boiler shop, where hand riveting had mainly been replaced by steam and hydraulic powered riveters. The same building contained the smithies, with 100 fires burning and where steam hammers of various sizes were used. This must have been the most deafening building in the entire works. The next buildings were the finishing and machine shops, where according to the account there was 'a bewildering profusion of machines of every description', all operated by belts from line shafting.

Midland Railway
800 Class 2-4-0 No. 1522 built by Neilson, 1879.

Next all the different parts were assembled in the erection shop, after which after being steam tested, the engines were passed on for painting before being sent on their way.

During those years, there had been several other major changes. James Reid had become a partner and in 1884, Neilson left to start a new business, the Clyde Locomotive Company. Between 1886 and 1888, they built thirty locomotives, fourteen of them for British lines and the rest going to South America. It was after that that they were bought out by Sharp Stewart. Although Reid was now in sole charge, the name Neilson was so well known and respected that it was kept on until 1898, when it became Neilson, Reid and Company. Among the many locomotives built during this time was a set of 2-6-0s for the Great Eastern, the first of this wheel arrangement to run in Britain. One of the engines was named *Mogul* – and the name came to be used for all locomotives of this type. The export trade continued to be of huge importance to the country and some of their largest

South Eastern Railway Class Q, No. 312, built c.1900 by Nielson.

0-4-4 Kirtley 690 Class, one of a batch of twenty built by Dübs in 1870.

engines were destined to go to overseas customers, including 4-8-0s, 4-6-4Ts and 4-10-2Ts for South Africa. A far from conventional engine was built in 1861 to haul sledges across the ice separating St Petersburg from Kronstadt. By the time the company ceased operating independently as it entered into the consortium that was to become North British in 1903, the work force had increased still further to 3,500 and output had risen to around 300 locomotives a year.

When Henry Dübs left Neilson, he set up his new works at Little Govan, now named Polmadie, to the south of the Clyde in Glasgow. The first locomotive to leave the works was an 0-4-2, one of a batch of ten for the Caledonian Railway. Although, like the other Glasgow builders, the company relied heavily on overseas orders, they also had some good regular customers in Britain. They built a number of very

B12 Class 2-6-0 locomotive for the Queensland Railway, built by Dübs c. 1880.

A Dübs locomotive of 1898 for the Abt system Mount Morgan rack railway in Australia.

fine locomotives for the Midland Railway, such as the elegant 1070 Class, designed by Samuel Johnson. Although most of the output was in the form of conventional locomotives, they did build a special engine for the Australian Mount Morgan rack railway that used the Abt system, developed in Switzerland. The company invested in the Canadian Locomotive & Engineering Works at Kingston, Ontario and took complete control in 1888. They relied heavily on orders from Canadian Pacific and Grand Trunk Railways, but when those companies began manufacturing their own engines the Dubs company went bankrupt. It was quickly revived by new investors.

The Canadian venture was not the only one to suffer from competition. All three Glasgow companies relied heavily on exports, but more and more orders were going to America.

New Zealand Railways F30 Class built by Dübs in 1880

Ben Class Number 1, Ben-y-Gloe built for the Highland Railway by Dübs in 1898.

Neilson may have been turning out around 300 locomotives a year at the beginning of the twentieth century, but the American giant Baldwin was building nearly 3,000 a year. The three companies – Sharp, Neilson and Dübs amalgamated to form the North British Locomotive Company. All the sites remained in use, and each had its own maker's name plate – circular for Hyde Park, oval for Atlas and diamond for Queens Park. This did not mean that any particular works was concentrating on one specific type of locomotive. One of the advantages of the merger was that if a large order came through it could be despatched more quickly by sharing it out around the different sites. In many other ways, it was

C13 Class 2-8-0 locomotive by Dübs, heading a coal train at the Noble Valley Colliery Bundamba, Queensland.

business as usual with locomotives for the home market and around the globe. These included a number of especially large engines for India, including 4-8-0s and 2-8-4Ts.

As with all British manufacturers, the advent of war in 1914 brought many changes, with parts of the works being devoted to producing armaments and ammunitions, though there was still a demand for locomotives from the War Department, and from India and France. After the war, it was decided to rationalise production by concentrating erection on just two sites – Queen's Park and Hyde Park – and the last locomotive left Atlas in 1923. A number of innovative designs were introduced at this time, including 0-6-6-0 Mallard locomotives for the Madras & Southern Mahratta Railway. These were based on the original design by the Swiss engineer Anatol Mallet. High pressure steam from the boiler is used to drive the rear, rigidly mounted drive wheels. The exhaust steam is then passed to the larger low-pressure cylinders to drive the front wheels, mounted on a bogie. The result is a form of articulated compound engine.

Other unusual engines were not always so successful. In 1910, they built a Reid-Ramsay electric locomotive. A conventional

Natal Government Class c 4-10-2 tank locomotive by North British, built in 1899.

boiler produced steam that turned an impulse turbine linked directly to a dynamo that generated the current to drive four 275hp motors. Nothing more was heard of this arrangement until 1924, when a second Reid-Ramsay type locomotive was built for showing at the British Empire Exhibition at Wembley. The frame of the 1910 engine was used but everything else was changed. The wheel arrangement was now 4-2-2-2-2-4. This was a condensing engine with two three-stage turbines, with the high pressure driving the trailing wheels and the low pressure the leading wheel. It was given a trial run in

South India Railway 4-4-2T, built by North British in 1920, seen here at Mysore.

Scotland but, although it worked, the performance was not satisfactory. The tractive effort produced was below that of a conventional steam engine of the same weight.

Another experimental engine, *Fury*, was built in 1929 for the LMS and designed by their chief mechanical engineer Henry Fowler, working in partnership with the Superheater Company. This was a high pressure compound 4-6-0 with one high pressure cylinder between the frames and two outside low pressure. The novel part was the three-stage boiler in which the special high pressure section was constructed of nickel-steel in Sheffield and had to withstand pressure up to 1,800psi. The first two stages were used in sequence to produce steam at a working pressure of 900psi, while the third stage was a conventional firetube boiler. The engine was given several trial runs, on one of which from Glasgow there was an explosion in the firebox, which killed the Superheater Company inspector. Tests failed to reveal what had caused the explosion, the boiler was repaired and more trials conducted. The results were never very satisfactory. It was later converted by William Stanier to a more conventional steam locomotive. A far more conventional set of locomotives for the LMS was the Royal Scot class, of which fifty were built by North British.

The 1930s saw a number of important overseas orders, including some very large engines, such as the 4-6-2s for the Nizam Government State Railway and 4-8-2s for South African Railways. During the Second World War the company continued to build locomotives, and during the period from 1943 to 1944 constructed 150 2-10-0 Austerity engines. At the end of the war, a number of large orders came through, one of which was for the LNER B1 Class. These 4-6-0 mixed traffic locomotives were designed by Edward Thompson in 1942, but North British only began construction in 1946. Between then and 1952, however, the works turned out 290 of these extremely useful engines. Among the outstanding overseas orders were for 100 of the 4-8-2 1F Class for the 3ft 6in gauge

The replica of Robert Stephenson's Rocket at Tyseley.

The replica of *Der Adler*, Germany's first locomotive, in the DB Museum Nuremberg.

***L'Aigle* in** the Musée de Train, Mulhouse

Great India Peninsula Railway WCG1 at Delhi.

Manning Wardle saddle tank *Sir Berkeley* of 1896 at the Middleton Railway.

Kitson *Fairy* *Queen*, built for the East India Railway in 1855, seen here with an excursion train at Delhi in 2017.

Kitson steam tram, one of eight supplied to the Christchurch Tramway Company, New Zealand between 1879 and 1881, seen here at Ferrymead Heritage Park.

A Kitson HGS Class 2-8-0 of 1914, now owned by Pakistan Railways, heading an excursion train at the Khyber Pass.

Hunslet 0-4-0ST *Elidir* of 1889 on the Llanberis Lake Railway.

Hunslet saddle tank No.4 at Java Sugar Works.

***Left*: New Zealand** EW Class electric locomotive at Ferrymead Heritage Park.

***Below*: Sharp Stewart** B-Class locomotives getting up steam for a day's work on the Himalaya Darjeeling Railway.

New South Wales Beyer Garrett AD60 4-8-4+4-8-4 near Wagga Wagga.

***Right*: Bagnall 2-4-0T** *Polar Bear* of 1905 at Amberley Working Museum.

***Below*: Aveling & Porter's** last locomotive, *Blue Circle*, built in 1926, at Shackerstone on the Battlefield Line.

Replica of *John Molson*, built by Kinmet, Hutton & Steel for the Montreal & Lachine Railroad.

Locomotive No. 12
Sarah Siddons built for the Metropolitan Railway by Metropolitan Vickers in 1921.

De Winton locomotive *Chaloner* of 1877 at Leighton Buzzard.

Former War Department Austerity 4300 Class 2-8-0 photographed in Holland.

South Africa Railways. With 14,000 route miles, this is the most demanding narrow gauge network in the world, and created a need for powerful locomotives. In 1951 there was another order for 100, even bigger, 4-8-4 engines for South Africa. At the same time another 100-engine order came for 4-6-2s for the 1m gauge Indian State Railway. But in the 1950s, production was steadily being shifted from steam to diesel and electric locomotives.

The first diesel was originally ordered by LMS but was only delivered in 1950 to newly nationalised British Rail. After that, they provided eight Bo-Bo diesel electrics for the

Ceylon Government railway. A one-off 0-8-0 or D hydraulic diesel was delivered to the 3ft 6in gauge Emu Bay Railway in Tasmania, which is now preserved in that country. But unlike their plethora of orders from overseas for steam engines, they never had the same success with diesels. Instead, they began building locomotives for British Rail. The diesel engines were designed by the German engineering company MAN. A number of Classes were supplied, starting with the Class D3/1 diesel hydraulic. They were not a success – and many ended up being returned to the works for repair. There was a particularly worrying problem that occurred when exhaust fumes filtered through into the cab at serious risk to the driver. Not surprisingly, the hoped for large orders never materialised.

The first venture into electric traction came when the General Electric Company agreed to build forty locomotives

Type 4 diesel-hydraulic supplied to the Western Region of British Rail in 1958, seen here at Reading.

for South Africa. They would supply the power unit, but the locomotives would be built at North British. The two companies co-operated again, this time building engines for the West Coast main line electrification programme of the 1960s. These became the Class 84, but only ten were ever built and no more were ordered, as, like the diesels, they proved unreliable in service. The failure to make headway into the post-steam age led to the eventual closure of the company in 1962. It was a sad end to a company that had supplied the whole world with magnificent locomotives for more than 100 years.

Chapter Seven

Beyer Peacock

We first met Charles Beyer when he was employed at Sharp Stewart. He was born in Germany and studied engineering there, but in relation to the cotton industry not railways. He came to England in 1831 at the age of 21 and joined Sharp Roberts as a draughtsman at the time when they were mainly manufacturing textile machinery and remained with them until 1853, by which time he had become their chief engineer. Richard Peacock was apprenticed to the pioneering locomotive company Fenton, Murray & Jackson in 1834. He must have been an extraordinarily bright apprentice, for just four years later he was made locomotive superintendent for the Leeds & Selby Railway Company. He was to go on to work with a number of different companies, including a brief spell under Daniel Gooch at Swindon. He became locomotive superintendent for the Manchester, Sheffield & Lincolnshire Railways in 1847 and that was also the year that he first met Charles Beyer. Seven years later, in 1854, they joined forces to found Beyer Peacock. The company was to become famous for manufacturing the Beyer-Garratt locomotives, but there was to be half a century of highly successful locomotive construction before that.

The 12-acre site for the new works, the Gorton Foundry, was at Openshaw, two miles from the centre of Manchester. Construction began in 1854. Beyer was in charge of setting up the works with its essential array of machine tools, and the first locomotive was a 2-2-2 for the GWR that was delivered in 1855. That year they employed 350 workers, but the numbers steadily grew until at their peak in the 1930s, they were employing around two and a half thousand.

Prinz August built by Beyer for the Swedish State Railway in 1856.

Although they were to continue to manufacture for British companies, many of their main customers were overseas, particularly British colonies, though there were also engines built for European countries. Among their first orders were locomotives for Great North of Scotland, the Edinburgh & Glasgow, the South Staffordshire, East Indian and the Swedish State railways. The latter was a B-Class 2-4-0 passenger locomotive, *Prinz August*, completed in 1856. It has been preserved and is now in the Swedish Railway Museum in Gavle. It is still in working order, though it has not been steamed for several years. As can be seen from the photo on the previous page, it is a handsome machine with elegant lines, characteristics that were to be the hallmark of Beyer Peacock locomotives. Their most important European connection, however, was with the Netherlands. A number of their locomotives have been preserved, but they are only a fraction of the whole. By far the biggest number were 2-4-0s in many different classifications, with the 1300 class – the 'big greens' – the most numerous at 182, then the 700 Class at 75 and 50 of the 900 Class. In the latter part of the nineteenth century and the early years of the twentieth they supplied smaller numbers of larger engines – 4-4-0 s, 4-4-2s, 4-6-0s and 4-6-4s. It is not unreasonable to say that in the nineteenth century, railways in the Netherlands were totally dominated by Beyer Peacocks.

Among the more interesting locomotives developed for the home market were the engines specially designed for London's Metropolitan Railway. As described earlier, the first attempt to solve the problem of choking steam and smoke in the underground sections of the line was 'Fowler's Ghost'. The first trains to run on the line had been broad gauge GWR, but when they withdrew, the company decided it needed its own locomotives and turned to Beyer Peacock. The A class made their first runs in 1864. They were 4-4-0 condensing tank engines. The idea for a condensing engine was not new – it had already been used on the GWR engines. Exhaust steam from the cylinders was fed through external pipes to tanks where it was condensed. The basic design was based on engines originally supplied to the Tudela-Bilbao Railway. There was still the problem of smoke, partially solved by changing from coal to coke. A second updated B Class was developed in 1879, and there were further changes, with coke being abandoned in favour of smokeless Welsh coal. The condensing locomotives continued to be used underground until electrification in 1905.

Among their other important developments were steam trams. Until the 1880s, British law would not allow steam to be used in any urban tramways which had to continue to rely on horses. Once the law had changed there was a flurry of activity, and one of the first to order steam trams was the North Staffordshire Tramway centred on Stoke-on-Trent. Beyer Peacock provided one of the first batch of steam trams in 1881 for the 4ft gauge line. It was a combined steam car and was given the number 5. A far more extensive system was developed in Lancashire. The Manchester, Bury, Rochdale & Oldham Tramway of 1883 was the longest tramway system in the world at the time, with over 53 miles of track. It did not, however, quite live up to the grandeur of its title, never actually reaching Manchester. This time the company provided locomotives not combined units., as they

The Oost-Java (East-Java) steam tramway opened in 1889. The train is seen here at Batavia.

continued to do for other steam tramways. They had a chance to extend their tram business overseas, when they received an order from the New South Wales Government Tramway. In 1885 they supplied an engine, *John Bull,* which, like other tram locomotives, had protective metal shielding to cover the wheels of the 0-4-0 engine. It had a vertical boiler and drove the wheels through reduction gear. It was fitted with Wilkinson's Patent Exhaust Superheater to reduce the smoke. It was heavier than the normal British tram locomotive but proved disappointing in performance and after just a few years was returned to Gorton where it was used for shunting. It has now been preserved at the tram museum at Crich, Derbyshire. Altogether, 200 tram engines were built. The biggest customers were in Java, with a total of 70 engines that included the 66 mile long East Java tramway.

Among the stranger railways for which the company provided locomotives was the Puerto Cabello and Valencia Railway in Venezuela. It was a mixed line, starting on the coast as a conventional railway and then followed a river valley to the foot of the coastal range of mountains. This involved a climb of 500m and the engineer John Carruthers incorporated a 4km section of rack railway based on the Abt system. This appears to have been the company's only rack railway to be served by the company.

South Australian 5ft 6in gauge J Class locomotive of 1874.

Beyer Peacock supplied locomotives to the Isle of Man 3ft gauge railway from its opening in 1874, half a dozen of which are still in use, among them No.5, *Loch*, a 2-4-0 of that year. To describe it as original would not be perhaps altogether true, as it has been reboilered several times and many working parts have been replaced. Nevertheless, it remains substantially just as it was designed a century and a half ago. There were important changes at the Gorton works, including the introduction of mild steel in construction that led the company to build its own steel foundry in 1899. In 1907,

London South Western Railway 302 Class, designed by William Beattie in 1876, photographed c.1890.

Midland Railway 2203 Class of 1893, from the *American Engineer and Railroad Journal.*

they produced their 5,000th locomotive and since the first engine had been rolled out, two thirds of locomotives had gone to overseas railways. They did, however, build many locomotives for leading British companies as well, including the Midland and the London South Western.

The twentieth century saw a number of changes, starting in 1902 when it became a limited liability company. An important individual began an association with the company shortly afterwards. Herbert William Garratt was a British engineer who had enjoyed a successful career in South America and returned to Britain in 1906 as locomotive superintendent for the New South Wales Government Railways, charged with inspecting locomotives to approve their export to Australia . During that time, he worked on the design for a new kind of articulated locomotive, for which he was granted a patent in 1908. The first manufacturer he approached was Kitson, but they were not interested. His next approach was to Beyer Peacock, who acquired the rights to the patent but did not rush to put his ideas into practice. They had already worked with articulated engines. They had built a Mallett for a 2ft gauge line in Tasmania, after which in 1908 they suggested supplying a Garratt. The engine had to be able to negotiate the sharp curves and often steep sections of the line, hence the need to have both a great deal of power, which could not be supplied by simply increasing the size of a conventional engine that would not be able to negotiate the bends – hence the need for an articulated locomotive.

There were three essential elements of the Garrat locomotive. The boiler was fitted to a girder frame with pivot points at either end. Below these pivot points were bogies carrying the engine components. The rear section usually contained fuel and water, the front usually just a water tank. There were many advantages to the Garratt system. A large boiler could be used, and there was ample space for a big firebox and ashpan, making them ideal for countries where they were required to work on long routes. The two bogies enabled them to spread the load when running on light rails and negotiate difficult curves. There was ample tractive effort for difficult, mountainous terrain. When Beyer Peacock sent the specifications for the first Garratt for Tasmania, they claimed the engines would be able to negotiate curves of 99ft radius and cope with inclines of 1 in 25. The Tasmanian Railway, however, demanded several changes from the original design they had been sent. Firstly, the engines had to be compounds, with two high pressure cylinders on the rear engine unit and the two larger low pressure cylinders on the front unit. They were also required to have the cylinders pointed inwards to shorten the distance that steam had to travel from high pressure to low pressure. Beyer Peacock complied with the requirements and the first two locomotives, which became the 0-4-0+0-4-0 K-Class were built in 1909. The first Beyer Garratts were a success, but the company only made one more compound engine and never used the inward pointing cylinders again.

The next order was for the Darjeeling Himalaya for two 0-4-0+0-4-0 locomotives that proved roughly 65 per cent

The K1 Garratt, the first articulated locomotive built by Beyer Peacock, supplied to the North-East Dundas Tramway in Tasmania in 1909.

more power than the existing 0-4-0 tank engines then in use on the line. The value of the new engines soon brought the company customers from around the world. They were to be found on every continent and in very many countries, the one notable exception being the United States. Arguments about just how efficient they were put to the test when a 3ft 6in gauge GA Class 2-6-0+2-6-0 Garratt was brought to South Africa in 1921. Trials were held on the line between Durban and Ladysmith that contains sharp curves and gradients up to 1 in 30. The competitors were a Class MH 2-6-6-2 Mallet and a conventional Class 14 4-8-2. The Garratt came out an easy winner on all counts. The 4-8-2+4-8-2 GL Class built for South Africa for the 3ft 6in gauge in 1929-30 were the most powerful Garratts built for any line. They were not, however, the largest – these were 4-8-2+4-8-2s built for the USSR in 1932 and weighing a massive 255 tons.

Several Beyer-Garratts have been preserved in museums around the world and Britain is fortunate to have them not only on static display but running. The Welsh Highland Railway owns several, including the historic K1 that started the whole

East African Railways 59 Class 4-8-2+2-8-4 Garrat photographed 1953.

story. I recently had the privilege of joining the footplate crew for the journey from Carmarthen to Porthmadog on a former South African engine, that still had the lettering in the cab in Afrikaans, a reminder of just how important Africa was to the company. Over the years, more than 1,000 of these engines were built, the last for South African Railways in 1958.

Like so many other companies, when the war broke out in 1914, the works began to switch from building locomotives to supplying heavy artillery. In 1915 the government took control of the works and artillery manufacture dominated. Locomotive production did continue during the Second World War, when production included large numbers of Garratts. The post war years, however, saw the steady replacement of steam by diesel and electric traction. The company decided to specialise in diesel-hydraulic engines, and although they received a few orders from British Rail the company began to founder when British Rail decided to concentrate on diesel-electric locomotives. The company finally closed down in 1966 after over a century of building locomotives to the very highest standard.

Chapter Eight

W.G. Armstrong

This is an unusual member of the locomotive construction fraternity in that this was never a major part of the company's business. William George Armstrong was born in Newcastle upon Tyne in 1810, where his father was a corn merchant. He, however, trained to be a solicitor, but took a keen interest in engineering and was a member of the Literary and Philosophical Society. In the 1840s he began developing a design for a hydraulically operated crane. In 1847, he established a small factory alongside the Tyne at Elswick on the west side of the city. He began manufacturing his crane with a workforce of just twenty. It was an immediate success and soon expanded and within ten years had turned out 1,000 cranes. In 1848, he designed a 2-2-2 condensing engine with a vertical boiler. Working drawings exist, but little more is known about this or of any other engines that were built at this time. In 1859, he made another highly successful move into armaments manufacture, establishing an ordnance factory, also at Elswick. In 1861, the company again began manufacturing locomotives in a small way, including twenty 2-4-0s for India. Production stopped again in 1868.

In 1897, Armstrong bought up the Whitworth factory in Manchester and formed a new company Armstrong Whitworth. He was also by now involved in shipbuilding on the Tyne, specialising in warships. Armstrong was given a peerage, becoming First Baron Armitage and died in 1900. He was not only an innovator, but very forward looking, advocating the end of using fossil fuels and turning to hydroelectric and solar power, remarkable at such an early date.

A 2-6-0 standard gauge locomotive for the Egyptian State Railway being loaded onto a ship at the Armstrong works in 1928.

In the First World War, the company had been heavily engaged with providing armaments, but as the war ended the Newcastle factory was converted to locomotive manufacture, and this time it was to remain in production for decades not years and was to earn a special place in British railway history, but not for their conventional steam locomotives, although they did produce a wide variety of locomotives for both home

Gresley designed London North Eastern Railway K3 2-6-0 at York in 1939, photographed by the late Walter Dandy.

and overseas railways. Their first order in 1919 was for fifty 0-6-0 engines for the North Eastern Railway, completed in 1921. That year, however, saw a much larger commission, and over the next two years, they built 200 2-8-0s for the Belgian State Railway. There were no more big orders until the 1930s, during which time they constructed a total of 337 Class 5 4-6-0s for the London, Midland & Scottish, the famous Stanier Black Fives. One class of engines does, however, deserve a special mention. In the 1920s, the South Australia Railway was undergoing a modernisation programme that included upgrading part of the old narrow gauge to 5ft 3in gauge. They needed powerful engines to cope with the steep gradients of the Adelaide Hills, and the answer was the 500 Class of 4-8-2s that were built at Armstrong- Whitworth in 1926, the biggest non-articulated locomotives ever built in Britain.

In 1922, the company began an interesting experiment in producing a mainline locomotive that would be powered by an electric motor, but which would not require the expensive infrastructure required to provide the current, such as overhead lines. Instead, the engine would generate its own

South Australia
500 Class, 4-8-2
No. 502 *James Maguire* c.1925.

electricity. The Ramsay turbo-electric engine was constructed in two sections. In the first was a boiler raising steam to drive a turbine that would power the generator. The section had two electric motors and a 2-6-0 wheel arrangement The rear section held the coal and water and had six coupled wheels, also powered by electric motors. The engine was given trials but although they seem to have been successful, it was never put into service and no similar engines were built. In the 1930s, the company changed course, abandoned the steam turbine and began developing diesel electric shunters and railcars.

The Swiss company Sulzer had developed a diesel engine for use with main line locomotives in 1912, but it had not been entirely successful and was difficult to start. In the 1920s they developed smaller engines that could be used, for example, for railcars. In 1931 Armstrong-Whitworth made

The erecting shop at Armstrong Whitworth, from a company photograph, published in 1931.

an arrangement with the Swiss company to make their diesels under licence, and work began on their first diesel-electric rail car, *Tyneside Venturer*. The engine was a 6-cylinder, 4-stroke engine delivering 250 horse power. It was mounted beneath the forward driving cab and drove the generator that provided the electricity for two General Electric motors. The rail car had a rear driving compartment, and in between were two vestibules each seating 25 passengers. The riveted steel bodywork was supplied by Cravens Railway Carriage & Wagon Co. of Sheffield. The designed top speed was 65mph. After extensive trials, the railcar was bought by LNER at the end of 1932. In service in the north of England it ran for over 30,000 miles with average fuel consumption figures that would make a modern motorist wince – just under 5 miles per gallon.

Three other railcars were later built, and a lighter rail bus with a 95hp engine and coachwork by Park Royal of London.

TURBO-ELECTRIC CONDENSING LOCOMOTIVE.

GAUGE 4′ 8·5″ FACTOR OF ADHESION 11·05′.

TRACTIVE FORCE 22,000 LBS.

WORKING PRESSURE–200 LBS. PER SQ. IN.

WHEEL DIAMETERS	COUPLED	4′ 0″
	BOGIE	3′ 1″
WHEEL BASE	RIGID	16′ 4″
	TOTAL	59′ 4″
		Tons
WEIGHTS	BOILER VEHICLE	67·25
	CONDENSER VEHICLE	63·5
	TOTAL	130·75
	ADHESIVE WEIGHT	108·5
HEATING SURFACE WITH SUPERHEATER		1453 sq. ft.
GRATE AREA		28.4 „ „
TURBO GENERATOR		890 K.W. at 3,600 revs. 27·5″ vacuum.
TANK WATER CAPACITY		2500 Galls.
FUEL CAPACITY		4 Tons
VOLTAGE		600 volts.

REF. No. E 14.

LOCOMOTORA DE CONDENSACIÓN TURBO-ELÉCTRICA.

ANCHO DE VÍA: 1,43 METROS. FACTOR DE ADHERENCIA: 11,05.

ESFUERZO DE TRACCIÓN, 9.979 KGS.

PRESIÓN ÚTIL: 14,061 KGS. POR CM. CUADRADO.

DIÁMETROS DE LAS RUEDAS	ACOPLADAS	1,22 m.
	BOGIE	0,94 m.
DISTANCIA ENTRE LOS EJES	RÍGIDAS	4,98 m.
	TOTAL	18,08 m.
PESOS	VEHÍCULO DE CALDERA	68,32 ton.
	„ „ CONDENSADOR	64,51 „
	TOTAL	132,84 „
	ADHERENCIA	110,23 „
SUPERFICIE DE CALDEO CON RECALENTADOR		134,98 m²
SUPERFICIE DEL EMPARRILLADO		2,64 „
TURBO-GENERADOR		890 K.V. a 3.600 r.p.m. Vacío de 698,50 mm.
CAPACIDAD DEL DEPÓSITO DE AGUA		11365 lit.
CAPACIDAD DE COMBUSTIBLE		4,06 ton.
VOLTAJE		600 voltios.

No. DE REF. E 14.

29

An Armstrong advertisement aimed at the South American market.

It began operations at Coventry on 14 September 1936 and was fitted with pneumatic tyres, intended to give a uniquely smooth, silent ride, with a cruising speed of 55-60mph. In a report welcoming the service, the *Midland Daily Telegraph* quoted one satisfied passenger: 'This is just like riding at 70mph in the most luxurious motor car you can imagine along the top of a billiard table.'

In 1933 the company produced their first diesel-electric shunter fitted with the same power unit as the railcars. It had a 1-Co-1 wheel arrangement. The case for acquiring such engines was succinctly put on a label on the back of a photo of one of the first shunters. 'Although equipped with only

The Coventry railbus, developed by LMS, Michelin and Armstrong Siddeley in 1935.

a 250-bhp engine, tests have proved that it can carry out all duties previously performed by steam locomotives capable of developing 800 h.p. at a fuel cost of only 7 pence halfpenny to 8 pence per mile.' It was given extensive trials, and was to be the forerunner for a whole fleet of shunters that would be developed over the years.

By 1937, the international situation was looking increasingly grim. The company decided to return their Scotswood plant to armament manufacturing. There may have been other commercial reasons behind the change, as they had diversified considerably over the years, adding road vehicles and aircraft building to their other activities. They never returned to locomotive construction, but in their time they had built almost 1,500 engines and had been pioneers in the development of diesel traction.

Chapter Nine

W.G. Bagnall

The company was started by William Gordon Bagnall who worked for two years in a bank before joining his father's company, the John Bagnall & Sons ironworks at West Bromwich. He left his father to form his own engineering company in 1875 when just 23 years old, taking over a small milling business that was to become the Castle Engine Works, Castleton, Stafford. At first, they were simply involved in general engineering practice, providing a wide range of products serving everything from agriculture to the coal industry. They built their first locomotive, an 0-4-0 saddle tank, in 1876, and building small industrial locomotives, especially tank engines, was to be their main stock in trade throughout the steam period. There was, however, a difference in their early locomotives; what would normally be thought of as a saddle tank was instead wrapped round the underside of the boiler and supported the firebox.

Samuel T. Price joined the company in the late 1880s, an experienced engineer who had previously been employed at the Midland Railway's Derby works. He was to be mainly responsible for design of locomotives. Mostly, they used standard systems, but they also developed their own valve gears. The first was designed by the company's chief draughtsman, Ernest E. Baguley and was a rocking type, in which a third rod was attached to the crank pin between the connecting and coupling rods. It was first used in 1893 on an 0-4-0 tank engine for the Northern Outfall Works at Beckham. In 1903 another different valve gear, the Bagnall-Price, was introduced. This was an adaptation of the well-known Walschaerts gear and was simpler than

An 0-6-0 saddle tank No. 2994 Vulcan at Bishop's Lydeard on the West Somerset Railway c.1980.

the Baguley. They also used circular marine boilers on some narrow gauge locomotives. In 1924 they built the first of several fireless locomotives, in which the steam was supplied from an outside source and stored in a cylindrical reservoir on the engine. It was supplied to the 2ft 6in gauge line serving Edward Lloyds paper mill at Sittingbourne in Kent. Altogether ten fireless locomotives were built.

They continued to specialise in light and narrow gauge locomotives right up to 1926, when they received an order for a number of 0-6-0 tank engines for the GWR and Somerset & Dorset railways. In the 1930s they bult fifty 0-6-0 pannier tanks for the GWR. The same period saw the company moving into diesel production. Their first order was from the

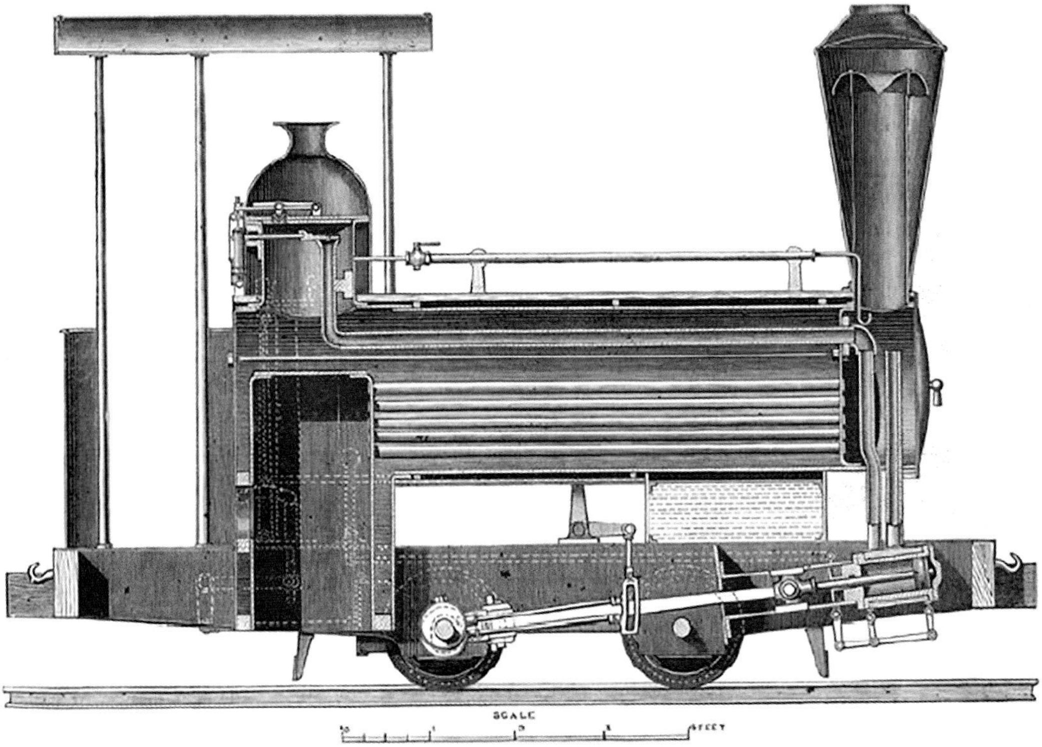

An inverted saddle tank locomotive built in 1879 for Puerto Rico, from *The Engineer*, November 1880.

Ashanti Goldfields in South Africa, where the 2ft line included curves with tight 60-foot radius curves. The engine was articulated, carried on two 4-wheel bogies. This was followed the next year, by an articulated 0-4-0+0-4-0 steam locomotive for a 2ft 0½in gauge line at a sugar estate, also in South Africa. In many ways it resembled a Garratt, but there were significant differences. The rear power bogie was set directly under the firebox. As a result, a circular 'bull head' marine boiler replaced the more conventional locomotive type. The locomotive company also used their own patent fastener to connect the flexible tubes for steam and exhaust pipes. Their last steam locomotive was constructed in 1957, a 2-8-2 narrow gauge engine for the Mysore Iron and Steel Works in India.

After completing their first diesel, Bagnall signed an agreement with the Deutz motor manufacturers of Cologne

Egyptian Delta Light Railway 0-6-4 tank engine taking on water in 1945.

The 0-4-4-0 Monarch of 1953, seen here on the Welshpool & Llanfair Light Railway

to secure the sole rights for using their engines in Britain. They later constructed a few electric locomotives and in 1951, with steam engine demand fading away, the company went into association with Brush Electrical Engineering to become Brush-Bagnall Traction Ltd.

Charles Frederick Brush invented an electric dynamo in 1876 and set up an Anglo-American company. The American end was sold off to General Electric and the British branch, the Brush Electric Light Company, moved to new premises in Loughborough in 1881 to manufacture electric motors. To see how they came to be involved in locomotive manufacture, we need to take another step back in time.

Henry Hughes started his working life as an engineer and timber merchant and in 1865 he acquired a site next to the Midland Railway lines in Loughborough that became the Falcon Works. He used his experience in the timber trade to begin constructing wooden coaches and trucks. Exactly when he began making locomotives is uncertain, but in 1867 he displayed a 0-4-0 saddle tank at the Paris Exhibition. In the 1870s they began supplying tram engines, but unlike other manufacturers, they did not provide completely new designs, merely adapted their standard tank engines by converting them to condensing engines and providing metal plating on the outside to cover the working parts. One of these, *The Pioneer,* was the first locomotive to work the Swansea & Mumbles tramway, a line that had been worked by horses since its opening in 1804. The company was never a great success. In 1887 Hughes left and it was taken over and renamed Falcon Railway Plant Works, under the direction of Norman Scott Russell. In 1889 the company was taken over by Brush and renamed Brush Electric Engineering, continuing to make steam locomotives at the site until the end of the First World War.

During the war years, they began manufacturing 2ft gauge battery electric locomotives, known as 'tractors' and when the war ended several were sold off as war surplus. Two of these engines are still at work on the Hythe Pier Railway in Kent. In

1959 Brush-Bagnall merged with Dorman Diesel, a company originally formed to manufacture tools for the footwear industry but began manufacturing diesel engines in 1903. During the First World War they supplied 2- and 4-cylinder engines for the rail tractors on the 2ft gauge lines, for which Brush-Bragnall had supplied the battery tractors. The arrangement was short lived, as they were taken over by English Electric in 1962. The rest of that story has already been told in Chapter 5.

Ernest Baguley had been one of the key men at Bagnall and when he left he worked for a number of companies before forming one of his own in 1911 as Baguley (Cars) Ltd. As well as building motor cars, they reached an agreement with the Drewry Car Co. to start building rail cars. At the outbreak of war, Baguley joined the army, rising to the rank of major. After the war, the company continued their association with Drewry, but in 1919 they were in the process of building a petrol locomotive but were unable to obtain several essential components, so rather than let the machine languish in the

The Hythe Pier Railway is a 2ft gauge line built in 1909 but electrified in 1922. The train is hauled by one of the original electric engines.

workshop, they converted it to steam. They were to continue making steam locomotives, mainly 0-4-0 tank engines, though they also supplied the power units for nine steam railcars. They also continued building diesels until 1931, when the company went into liquidation.

To conclude this complex tale of mergers and takeovers, we can look at the continuing activities of the Brush group. Brush Traction was formed in 1951, specifically to build diesels for British Rail as they moved away from steam. They built engines in a variety of different classes for both mixed traffic and freight. In 1990, working with the Swedish company ABB, they began developing dual-voltage electric locomotives in readiness for the opening of the Channel Tunnel, so that they could be used on both sides of the Channel. The Class 92 was a freight engine. They also built the Eurotunnel Class 9 for use with the car shuttle service, with a designed top speed of 160km/hr. It was to be the last major development by the company. The Loughborough site was closed down in 2021.

A Eurotunnel Class 9 locomotive.

Chapter Ten

London Manufacturers

London investors had not exactly rushed to support the notion of steam engines for the world of transport. Richard Trevithick had tried to persuade them to put money into developing his steam road carriage and later demonstrated his *Catch-Me-Who-Can* locomotive at a site near the present Euston station. No one showed any interest. This is not, perhaps, too surprising. The steam locomotive was eventually to be promoted by men who needed efficient transport to move coal between mines and navigable waterways. The first London manufacturers were, as mentioned in Chapter 1, Braithwaite & Ericsson – later Braithwaite & Milner. It was a short-lived venture. They became bankrupt in 1839 but completed their final orders in 1841. The most unusual railway for which they supplied three 0-4-0 locomotives was the Allegheny Portage Railroad in America. It was part of a transport system linking Philadelphia to Pittsburgh. At both ends there were canals with horse-drawn passenger boats. These were not, however, ordinary boats. When it came to the Allegheny mountains, the boats were divided in two and floated onto wheeled carriages. These were then hauled up and down inclines on both sides of the hills, worked by stationary engines. The Portage Railroad linked the two inclines at the summit level. Rather cheekily, one of the locomotives they built for the Philadelphia & Reading Railroad was named *Rocket* after the famous engine that had defeated Braithwaite at Rainhill.

An unlikely name now features in the list of builders. Henry Maudsley is famous as a pioneer of machine tool manufacture from his works in Lambeth. He also manufactured steam engines after he had been joined in a partnership with Joshua Field, most famously providing the engines for Brunel's paddle steamer the *Great Western*. When he died in 1831, his sons carried on the business, and built twelve 0-4-0 tender locomotives for the London & Birmingham between 1838 and 1839 at their Lambeth works. These were the standard inside cylinder engines, designed by Edward Bury. There is no record of them building any more locomotives, though the company remained in business until the end of the nineteenth century.

The name George England is normally associated with the Ffestiniog Railway, but he was already building locomotives some years before the first for that line was constructed. England was born in Newcastle in 1811 or 1812 and his early career was spent in ship building in London. In the early 1840s he established the Hatcham Iron Works in New Cross to manufacture screw jacks and only began locomotive construction in 1846. He did, however, manufacture what the *Railway Times* called a 'manumotive railway carriage' in 1843 – a name that simply means that it was worked manually. It was an inspection car for use on the London & Croydon Railway that was said to be able to carry seven or eight passengers. In 1848, he built the first of a series of lightweight engines for use on the Newhaven Branch of the London & Brighton Railway. It was a 2-2-2 tender engine with 4ft 6in drive wheels and performed surprisingly well for its size; it weighed just 9 tons when carrying enough water and fuel for a 100-mile journey. It was eventually named *Little England* – the first of a class of Little Englanders. One of the class was shown at the Crystal Palace Exhibition of 1851 in a smart blue livery.

Only one of England's standard gauge engines has survived. This was an 0-4-0 well tank built in1857 for the Sandy & Potton Railway. It was later sold to the London & North Western (L&NWR) where it served for a time as a works shunter and was named *Shannon*. It then went to the Wantage Tramway in

George England locomotive No. 13 built for the Stockton & Darlington in 1864

1869 where the engine remained in service until the line was closed in 1946, though it had undergone several repairs and the cylinders had been replaced. It is now on display at the Didcot Railway Centre.

The main claim to fame for the company is, of course, its association with the Ffestiniog Railway – though the second "f" is a later addition. The line opened in 1836 to bring slate from Blaenau Ffestiniog down to the port of what was then Portmadoc. It was a challenging line, rising 700ft above sea level in 12 miles, with an average gradient of 1 in 92 and with several sharp bends. The gauge was just 1ft 11½in. This was not a problem in the early days. All the heavy traffic was downhill, and the horse that worked the line only had empty trucks to haul back up to Blaenau. In the early 1860s, the company's engineer and general manager Charles Spooner, decided that it was time to introduce steam onto the line. He approached George England probably because of his reputation for building lightweight but powerful engines.

George England
Wantage Tramway No. 59 of 1857 at Didcot Railway Centre.

Between 1863 and 1864 the company supplied four 0-4-0ST locomotives for the line, three of which *Princess, Prince* and *Palmerston* are still in use. Charles Spooner wrote his own account of these little engines in a book of 1879. One engine was unofficially known as 'the boxer', because the piston moved in short arm jabs and it ducked and weaved as it travelled. 'Over the old portions of the road a speed of 8 or 9 miles an hour is the greatest at which it is possible to run without incurring the risk of breaking the springs or loosening the driver's teeth.' This would seem to have been largely the result of poor track, rather than poor performance, as having travelled behind one of these venerable engines, I can confirm my teeth remained untroubled.

Originally the line was worked only for freight, but when it received the Board of Trade approval to carry passengers, there was an increase in traffic – with coaches of passengers being hauled uphill and not just empty waggons. It was felt

Welsh Pony, built by George England for what was then the Festiniog Railway in 1871.

that more powerful locomotives were needed. The Scottish engineer Robert Fairlie designed and patented his first double-ended locomotive *Pioneer* for the Neath & Brecon Railway in 1846. The engine had two back-to-back boilers, each carried on a powered 4-wheel bogie, with a central cab and firebox. It was built by James Cross & Co. of St. Helens in Lancashire. It was not entirely successful, largely due to problems with the firebox. This arrangement, however, seemed well suited to the needs of the Ffestiniog, spreading the load over eight wheels while still being able to negotiate tight bends, and the first locomotive was built by George England. Named *Little Wonder* it was built in 1869, and trials were begun testing the engine against the England 0-4-0 tanks. It proved superior, hauling trains of twice the weight of the standard tank engines.

In 1869, George England retired. He had the reputation of being a harsh employer and the entire workforce had indeed

The double-ended Fairlie Little Wonder on the Festiniog in 1871.

gone on strike for a short time in 1865, complaining about their conditions. Robert Fairlie took over the works, running them in conjunction with George England Jnr. They continued making Fairlie double locomotives, not only for the Ffestiniog but also providing engines for lines in France and Sweden. This period in the company's history was short lived. George England Jnr. died unexpectedly and the company closed down in 1872. Although most railway enthusiasts will always associate the company with the Fairlies, these represented a very small proportion of their output. The vast majority of the engines they built were 2-4-0s and 0-4-2 tanks, mainly to British companies but also sending engines to Belgium and Australia.

There is a curious footnote to this story. Robert Fairlie had actually eloped with England's daughter and they were married in France, where Fairlie claimed to have obtained her father's permission for him to marry the 18-year old. England was furious and tried to have Fairlie tried for perjury. It was only then that it was revealed that England had actually left his wife and he and 'Mrs. Fairlie', the girl's mother, were not actually married. In English law a baby born out of wedlock officially was registered as having no parents. As a result, Fairlie had no official parents he could ask for permission to marry the daughter and the case was dropped. Apparently the two families were reconciled.

The story of Merryweather & Sons begins when in 1836 Moses Merryweather took over a company started by Nathaniel Hadley in 1690 to manufacture firefighting equipment. By 1791, the company had been established as Hadley, Simpkin & Loot with new premises in Bow Street. Merryweather opened new premises in Greenwich, where he continued making fire engines, using a vertical steam boiler designed by Edward Field. With the latter's arrival, the name was changed to Merryweather & Field. They continued manufacturing firefighting equipment throughout the company's history but became interested in a new area in the 1870s – the steam tram.

Although urban steam trams had been in use in America for some time, British legislation prevented them being developed in this country on most routes, where they were governed by Acts mainly intended to prevent traction engines breaking up road surfaces. These include the famous – or infamous depending on one's point of view – Red Flag Act, that limited speeds to 4mph and required a man to walk in front with a red flag. In 1870 these restrictions were removed, but new restrictions were introduced. Speed had to be limited by a governor that would automatically cut off steam at 10mph, there had to be no emissions of smoke or steam and working parts had to be covered to within 4 inches from the ground. However, by a curious loophole in the legislation, the rules did not apply to tramways running alongside roads, an early example of which was the Wantage Tramway.

When the GWR came along, they refused to make a diversion to locate a station in the town, but instead built Wantage Road, 2½miles away. The first connection was by a horse drawn omnibus, but in the 1870s, local citizens raised the money for a roadside tramway. It was on this line that the first steam tram that involved the Merryweather company was to run. They supplied the power unit. It was designed in 1872 by the British engineer John Grantham, who had enjoyed a varied career, at first as a naval architect and engineer, then as engineer to the Buenos Aires Northern Railway, after which he returned to Europe, where he was in charge of constructing a horse-drawn tramway in Copenhagen. The Wantage vehicle was a double-decker 4-wheeled tram with the engine in the centre. Steam was supplied by two vertical Field boilers and the engine was under the floor, with two cylinders, driving one pair of wheels. It could be driven from either end. The London trials showed that the Field boilers were not suitable and they were replaced by a single boiler by Shand Mason & Co. who were to go on to supply boilers for many Merryweather trams over the next few years. It eventually began operations at Wantage in 1876.

The Merryweather company may have had only a minor role to play in the Wantage tram, but they recognised that this could be a useful adjunct to their main business. They did not follow the Grantham plan of integrating the power unit into the tram but built separate tram locomotives. After a few experiments they settled on a basic design, with horizontal boilers and inside cylinders. They either had steam condensers on the roof or fed the exhaust steam into a tank in the smoke box and then ejected it up the chimney. They developed six standard types, varying in weight from a 4-ton with 6in by 9in cylinders to a 9½-ton with 10in by 14in cylinders. In 1874, they delivered a single tram engine to Vienna, but in 1874, they began building engines for the Parisian tram network and by 1877 they had supplied them with forty-six trams. Overseas orders continued to be an important part of their work, supplying engines to many countries, with Rangoon and New Zealand being particularly important. Their biggest

Merryweather street tram at Wellington, New Zealand, 1878.

Merryweather tram locomotive of 1889 for the Rhineland Tramway company.

British customer was the North London Tramways. Grantham had run an experimental tram on the system in 1873, but with no success. Merryweather supplied fourteen engines in 1885. Their last steam tram was built in 1892. They had also built a number of steam inspection cars, but 1892 marked the end of the company's railway connections.

1892 was not merely the end of the Merryweather connection with steam trams. The whole system was to succumb to a rival form of power. In 1884 electric trams taking their power from an overhead supply began running on the Frankfurt-am-Main and Offenbach system. This was to be the favoured tram system from then onwards.

One London manufacturer had a small, but very interesting output. William Bridger Adams' father had been in the coach manufacturing business and in 1837 the son wrote a treatise on coach construction, which goes some way in explaining his later interests. In 1843 he set up his own Fairfield works at Fairfield Road, Bow. He developed an alternative to the scarf joint for joining rails. This used a fishplate joint and he took out a patent with a colleague, Robert Richardson, in1847. The device was adopted by the Eastern Counties Railway and his connection with that company brought him his first commission for a vehicle, a manually operated inspection carriage.

The next obvious move was to design a similar lightweight carriage but powered by steam not manpower. In collaboration with James Samuel, he designed a carriage capable of carrying seven passengers. It was a slightly curious 0-2-2T with a small vertical boiler, a tiny engine and a tank holding just 40 gallons of water. It was, however, a success, and encouraged Adams to move on to a much larger passenger vehicle *Fairfield* in 1848, which brought together the locomotive and passenger compartment as a single unit, thus making it a very early version of a railcar. It was initially built to standard gauge but was sold to the Bristol & Exeter Railway and had to be converted to 7ft gauge. A standard gauge version *Enfield* was built for the Eastern Counties with a 2-2-0 wheel arrangement and with a four-wheeled carriage attached to the outside frame that ran from the buffer beam on the engine to the rear of the coach. It could carry 42 passengers in four compartments. The long wheel base sems to have presented problems. For the next version for Eastern Counties. Adams built a Cambridge, that again had separate locomotive and carriage. He also built three conventional locomotives, two 0-2-2 and one 2-2-0 well tanks, all for Irish railways. It is not certain when the works closed, but Adams had in any case found a new interest in designing clothes and journalism. He died in1872.

Three more companies are known to have built locomotives in the London area. Adam Gordon of Deptford Green were primarily marine engineers, but there are references to at least two engines being built there. One was simply described as a 'small engine' that was given a trial on the London & Croydon Railway in 1839 and the company asked to hire it. There is some uncertainty with the next company, Appleby Bros of Southwark, who were general engineers producing a wide range of products. They are credited with building a 2ft 8in gauge 0-4-0T engine in 1839, but James W. Lowe suggests that although they designed it, the locomotive might have been built elsewhere. Christie Adams & Hill of Rotherhithe built six 2-2-2 locomotives for the L&SWR with 6ft 6in drive wheels.

The Adams railcar of 1849.

Chapter Eleven

Rail and Road

Several important manufacturers were at least as well, and possibly better, known for their road vehicles as they are for their locomotives. Thomas Aveling was one of the pioneers of traction engine development. He had a millwrighting business in Rochester, and he witnessed many portable steam engines at work in the surrounding countryside and he was not impressed: 'It is an insult to mechanical science to see half a dozen horses drag along a steam engine, and the sight of six sailing ships towing a steamer would not be more ridiculous.' He acquired a stationary engine from Clayton and Shuttleworth in 1859 and adapted it by means of a chain drive to a crankshaft on the rear axle to turn it into a traction engine. It was the start of a profitable business but in order to expand he formed a partnership with Richard Porter in 1862. Aveling & Porter went on to build traction engines and are best known for developing the steam roller. In 1864, they built the first traction engine designed to be run on rails instead of the road. One reason for the move may well have been the difficulty in steering the early traction engines, which had a single wheel in front, moved by means of a tiller – a difficulty they were only able to overcome when they began building steam rollers. There are no steering problems on railways.

The first engines were simply traction engines set on flanged wheels, in which the single cylinder was placed on top of the boiler, and power was transmitted via a countershaft and chains to gearing on the two axles. They were rated at 10hp. Over the years, the basic traction engine design was developed, in some cases by using a chain to couple the two axles. Engines of different sizes were produced, the largest being a 20hp version. They could be supplied with one or two cylinders and compound versions were also introduced and the drive could be supplied directly through gears to a crankshaft. They were slow but powerful, able to cope with gradients as steep as 1 in 20. One of the distinctive features was the solid wheels, which were in use on all engines until the 1920s, when spoked wheels were introduced. The company also developed tram engines in collaboration with Alfred Greig.

The last locomotive built by the company was works No. 9449 of 1926. It was supplied to the Holborough Cement Co, who were later taken over by Blue Circle, at which time the locomotive was given the company name. It is currently at the Nene Valley Railway, where it is being restored. The oldest surviving Aveling & Porter was built in 1872 for the Oxford & Aylesbury Tramway, later the Brill branch line. The small engine loped along in its working days at a leisurely 4mph and is now on static display at the Buckinghamshire Railway Centre. It is interesting to compare this modest locomotive with another exhibit there, *Sydenham* of 1895, a compound engine with a 7x13in high pressure and a 13x13in low pressure, both mounted above the boiler. The company continued in business after they stopped locomotive construction, mainly concentrating on steam rollers.

John Fowler established his works in Leeds in 1850. As well as constructing traction engines, he developed the first successful steam ploughing system. He died in an accident in 1864, but the firm continued to operate under Robert Fowler and two years later they began building locomotives, and the works became known as the Steam Plough & Locomotive Works. Unlike other traction engine builders, they did not adapt their original engines by adding flanged wheels but built conventional locomotives. In their first year they built an impressive twenty-two locomotives – 0-6-0s for the Chatham & Dover, 2-4-0Ts for the Waterford & Kilkenny, 2-4-0s for the

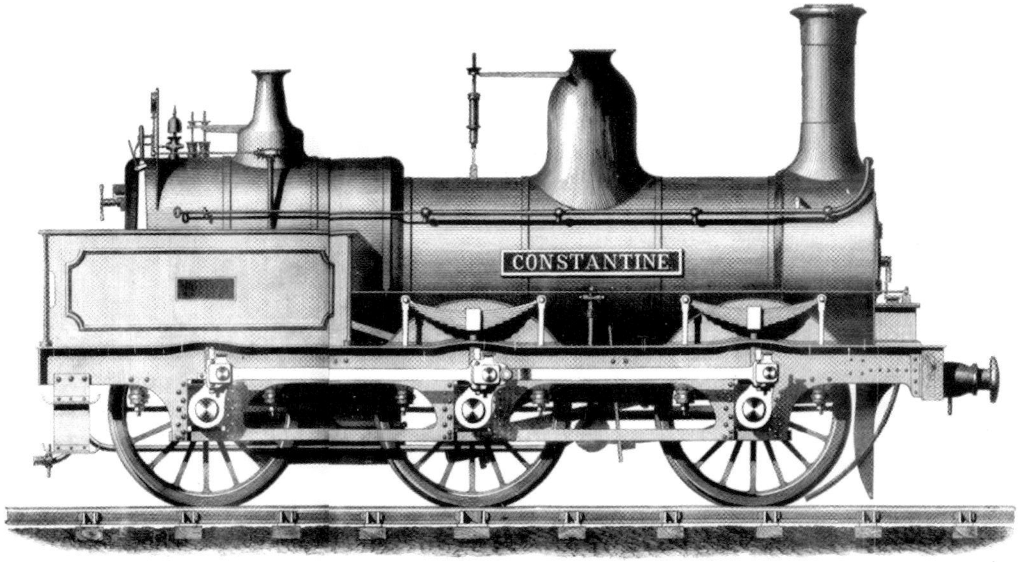

Fowler 0-6-0 built for the London, Chatham & Dover Railway in 1868.

Great Northern and their first export order, eleven 2-4-0s for the Imperial Mexican Railways. The next four years were taken up with constructing their range of 0-6-0 engines, the main customer being the Great India Peninsula Railway, who took a total of forty. They continued manufacturing standard gauge engines until 1856, when they completed an order for six 0-6-0STs for the Brecon & Merthyr Tydfil Junction Railway. But already they had started building narrow gauge locomotives, and this was to be their entire output for many years, supplying them for countries around the world. They mainly concentrated on four-wheel locomotives in different configurations and with different power ratings, from modest 18hp with 5½x10in cylinders to 190hp with 12x16in cylinders. They also built 0-6-2 tank engines specifically designed for wood burning.

Although they continued manufacturing steam locomotives until the 1930s, they increasingly turned to internal combustion engines. Their first power units were bought in from several different companies, but in 1923 they began building their own power units, the first being installed in 1923 in a 0-4-0

Fowler locomotive *Kate* of 1902, originally bought by the Colonial Sugar Refining Co., but seen here after having been taken over by the New South Wales Public Works Department.

petrol engine for the Nelson gasworks in Lancashire. This became the basis for a standard design, and in the 1930s they also began producing narrow gauge engines with a central driving cab. After the end of the war, they concentrated on standard gauge 150hp diesels, fitted with a variety of different power units. Throughout this period, they had continued providing agricultural engines and their crawler tractors were proving both popular and profitable. With limited manufacturing space available, they decided to discontinue the locomotive side of the business, and the last engine left Leeds in 1968.

Fowler 150hp diesel ordered by the Ministry of Works in 1939 for use by the RAF, seen here at Erwood Station in Wales.

The next manufacturer of steam road vehicles who turned to locomotive construction was Alley & MacLellan of the Sentinel Works in Glasgow. They manufactured marine steam engines among other things, and in 1903 they acquired Simpson & Bibby who had already begun manufacturing steam road vehicles at their works at Horsehay in Shropshire. In 1915, they opened a new factory at Shrewsbury, which was to become the sole manufacturer of steam vehicles and in 1920 became Sentinel Waggon Works Ltd.

The company's first steam wagon was built in 1905 and a year later they built their first 4-wheeled steam locomotives based on their road wagons. They were quite unlike conventional locomotives. A vertical water-tube boiler provided steam to two cylinders, from which the drive was transmitted by chain to the wheels. In the earliest versions, the cylinders were horizontal, but were vertical in the later models. They were intended mainly for shunting, for which the short wheel base made them particularly suitable and their exceptionally large water tanks meant that they could usually work all day without stopping for a refill. The standard model had a 100hp rating. They also manufactured an unusual two-cab version – the Y10 class for use by the LNER on their dock railways. As the engines had to run through streets, the working parts were covered as was normal for tram engines.

In 1923 they began constructing steam railcars, in association with Cammel Laird, later known as Metropolitan-Cammel, who supplied the coach work. The first was built for the narrow gauge Jersey railways & Tramways Co. In 1924, the LNER borrowed a rail car for a fortnight to give it a trial and were very satisfied with the result. Between1925 and 1942, they ordered eighty cars. Other companies also ordered railcars and they could be supplied in different forms, both single and double engine, with power ratings going from 100-125hp for a single car version to 350-400hp for the double.

The last steam locomotives were delivered in 1958, and the following year, the first diesel was sent to the Shropshire & Montgomery Railway, where it was well received and sixteen more were immediately ordered and delivered. Over the next five years, the company had developed four different classes, all powered by Rolls Royce engines. The original was a six cylinder 0-4-0 chain driven engine, followed by a heavier, eight cylinder 0-6-0 rod driven locomotive. They were successful, but the company later added two more, heavier, versions to the fleet. In 1967, the first of the Steelman Class was delivered to the Stewart & Lloyds steel works at Corby. This was a 600hp shaft driven 0-6-0 powered by the

Sentinel Tanganyika Railway metre gauge GSL Class.

Rolls Royce DV8T engine. Their most unusual locomotive was the electrogyro. It was developed for the National Coal Board as a fireproof engine, suitable for use underground. Where in an earlier age, a steam engine could receive steam from an outside source and store it in a reservoir to use, here the power was stored in a 3-ton horizontal flywheel, enclosed in a vessel filled with hydrogen under pressure to reduce resistance. It was initially powered by electric motors, fed from posts and would only be disconnected when the flywheel was up to speed. The engine was able to work for

Sentinel 4w No. 7492 built in 1928 for the Fry's chocolate factory in Keynsham.

about half an hour before it had to be recharged. Locomotive production stopped in 1971.

Clayton & Shuttleworth was established in Lincoln by Joseph Shuttleworth, and like other traction engine manufacturers, their first venture into locomotive construction, consisted of little more than adapting existing traction engines to run on rails as tram engines, but they also built a number of small shunting tank engines. In 1917, they established a new subsidiary, Clayton Waggons, specifically to take on railway work. Their early output was of vertically boilered geared locomotives, fitted with superheaters and working at 275psi. Two larger versions, with four vertical cylinders, were for the North Western Railway of India. The vertical boiler was also used in steam railcars, eleven of which were built for the London and North Eastern Railway and six for the Great Southern Railway of Ireland. The company later used the detached power section and adapted it to create a series of 0-4-0 shunting engines. The works were taken over and no more locomotives were built.

Three other traction engine companies built a small number of locomotives. Ruston Proctor were at established at the Sheaf Iron Works in Lincoln in 1857. They began making locomotives in 1866 and continued making small numbers for approximately the next twenty years. They were almost all conventional 0-4-0 and 0-6-0 tank engines, though one traction engine type was constructed in 1868. Their first customer was the Great Eastern, but from 1881 to 1886, their engines all went to Argentina, eighteen in all. Marshall of Gainsborough built three adapted traction engines between 1878 and 1902. Robey & Co. of Lincoln, best known for their steam rollers, built a number of tank engines for their own use, between 1876 and 1884 as well as a geared locomotive for South America.

CHAPTER TWELVE

More Scottish, Welsh Manufacturers and Irish Builders

We looked at some of the major Scottish constructors in Chapter 6, but they were by no means the only ones at work. One of the pioneers was the company founded by James and Charles Carmichael at the Ward Foundry, Dundee in 1810. Their first locomotive of 1833 was *Earl of Airlie,* a 0-2-4 for the 4ft 6½ in gauge Dundee & Newtyle Railway, an 11-mile-long line that included three rope-worked inclines. It was the first line to be built in northern Scotland. Surprisingly the engine survived long enough to be photographed. It shows a locomotive with two vertical cylinders, connected by a crosshead, with drive via a bell crank. They built a second engine for the line and that was their only venture into locomotive production, but they can claim the honour of being the first Scottish locomotive builders to supply engines for a Scottish railway.

Also from Dundee, James Stirling had originally begun training for a life in the church but was persuaded by his brother Robert to turn to engineering instead. Together they became partners in James Stirling & Co. at the Dundee Foundry. They supplied two locomotives to the Dundee & Newtyle line that were said to be very similar to the Carmichael engines. The line was later extended from Newtyle to Glamis as the Newtyle, Eassie and Glamiss Railway – Glamis was then spelt with an extra 's'. In 1838 they built a similar engine for the new line. Their next locomotives were very different. Five locomotives were built for the 5ft 6in gauge Arbroath & Forfar Railway

Andrew Carmichael locomotive *Earl of Airlie*, built in 1833 for the Dundee & Newtyle Railway.

between 1838 and 1840. The influence of Stephenson can clearly be seen. The outside cylinders were set at the firebox, inclining back at an angle to connect with the central drive wheel. In 1843, the company was taken over by Gourlay, Mudie & Co. who continued making five standard six-wheeled gauge locomotives for the Dundee, Perth & Aberdeen Junction Railway. They are believed to have built more engines, but no actual records survive to indicate what they might have been. Robert's son Patrick began his professional life as an apprentice at the firm, but was later to become famous as a designer, best known for the supremely elegant Stirling singles.

The next company to set up in Dundee was Kinmond, Hutton & Steed. Between 1838 and 1848, they built a large number of six-wheeled engines, all but three being 2-2-2s, the odd ones out being 0-4-2s for the Dundee, Perth & Aberdeen Junction. Their final batch for the Glasgow, Dumfries & Carlisle Railway were notable for their 6ft drive wheels. The only three not built for Scottish lines were sent to Canada, two to the Montreal & Lachine and one to the Champlain & St. Lawrence in 1847. The latter was named *John Molson* and a replica of this historic locomotive has been built (colour section).

Andrew Barclay had an interestingly mixed career before his company began manufacturing locomotives. He set up his first company at the age of 25 with Thomas McCullough manufacturing mill shafts at Kilmarnock in 1840. He patented a gas lamp, which he hoped would prove highly profitable, but sadly the money from the patent was never paid. In the meantime, he began manufacturing winding engines for local collieries, but without the gas lamp money, the business faltered. In 1859, he set up Andrew Barclay & Sons, and they began manufacturing locomotives at the Caledonia works. The company specialised in supplying locomotives for industrial sites, with a range of four and six-coupled tank engines, with distinctive square-sided tanks. They were highly successful and a large number of these sturdy locomotives have been preserved, with the largest collection, a total of eight, being at the Scottish Industrial Railway Centre at the former Duneskin Ironworks site in Ayrshire. Given the conservative nature of much of their output, it is surprising to find them constructing one very odd engine for the Caledonian Railway in 1871. It was a 2-2-2 locomotive but was fitted with a device designed by John Miller Ure, which allowed the drive wheels to be lifted off the track when the engine was coasting. Less surprisingly, it was not a success, and the engine was returned to a more conventional form.

One of their very successful lines was in fireless locomotives, which they began manufacturing in 1913. They proved particularly valuable when war broke out a year later for use in munition factories, where for obvious reasons every effort had to be made to reduce fire risks. The largest factory, in fact the largest of its kind in the world, was the Gretna factory. The work of that factory, which once employed 12,000 workers, nearly all women, is remembered in the Devil's Porridge Museum at Eastriggs. The name came from a description by Arthur Conan Doyle of the girls stirring the lumpy mixture that would become nitro-glycerine – 'stirring the devil's porridge'. Appropriately, the museum houses a Barclay fireless engine. What may well be the only working example of the 114 fireless engine they built is at the Scottish Industrial Museum.

Another successful line for the company was crane tanks, the first of which was completed in 1881. Most were built before 1910, but in 1942, they received an order from Clyde Alloy Steel. It was a dual-purpose machine, serving both as a conventional shunting tank engine and as a crane. It used

Andrew Barclay fireless engine of 1928 at the Scottish Industrial Railway Centre.

a steam driven turbine generator to provide electricity to power an electro magnet, used for picking up scrap metal. It is now housed at the Bo'ness and Kinneil Railway. As well as these special types, the company continued to supply a variety of locomotives for countries around the world. There was also a separate company, Barclays & Co., set up in 1872 for his four sons and his brother nearby at the River Bank works which concentrated on locomotive construction and seventy-six locomotives were known to have been bult there, before it was decided in 1888 that it was uneconomic to have two sites, and the Riverbank works closed and production returned to the original site.

Like many other companies, they saw that diesels were becoming an essential part of railway development, and they began construction in the 1930s, mainly building industrial shunters. Following nationalisation, they supplied a number of locomotives to British Rail, including the short wheel base 01, the D2/5 and the 06. In 1976, the company was taken over by the Hunslet group, who continued production at Kilmarnock as Hunslet-Barclay. Among their commissions were three-car trailer units for the Glasgow Metro. This circular underground 4ft gauge route was opened in 1896, using cable haulage, but the process of electrification began in 1923. There was a major modernisation programme begun in the 1970s and between 1992 and 1998, new central trailer three-carriage units were bult, with body shells completed by Hunslet in Leeds, and the engines and assembly at the Caledonia works.

The twenty-first century saw a flurry of changes. In 2007, it was taken over by Brush Traction and became Brush-Barclay and they in turn sold out to Wabtec Rail Scotland. The site is now owned by Brodie Engineering, and although locomotive construction has been discontinued the company still works at refurbishing existing stock.

It is rare to find a company specialising in just one type of locomotive, but that was the case of Alexander Chapman & Co.

The company was founded in 1849 as a general engineering company with a wide range of products including cranes and mechanical navvies. In 1860 they began building their own range of patented vertical boiler engines. The cylinders were attached to the boiler, above which was a guiding crosshead. The locomotives were all geared and mounted on two pairs of coupled wheels The design proved very successful and many were exported. Another Scottish company that became best known for one type of locomotive was Dick, Kerr & Co. It was founded in Kilmarnock by William Bruce Dick in 1854 in a quite unrelated field, dealing with oil refining and anti-fouling paint for ships, but in 1883 John Kerr joined the company and began locomotive manufacturing under the new name. They became particularly associated with steam tram engines, which included ten locomotives for the North

Chaplin locomotive built for the East London Harbour Railway in South Africa, photographed c.1890.

London Tramway in 1886-7. The tramway had originally been worked by horses and was the first London tramway to be successfully worked by steam. The steam trams became obsolete with the widespread introduction of electric trams, and Dick, Kerr was at the forefront of the new development. In 1893, they acquired new premises in Preston, Lancashire where they provided a variety of electrical equipment, especially for railway projects.

During the First World War, the works were largely given over to munitions, but they also produced 100 petrol-electric engines for the War Department. The four-cylinder petrol engine drove a 30kw DC generator. The engines could also be used as generators. At the end of the war, it was decided to sell off the Kilmarnock works, which were bought by the Kilmarnock Engineering Co., who continued at least into the 1920s with railway work, but there are no clear records of their production.

Dick & Stevenson was originally a foundry in Airdrie, begun in the 1790s by Alexander and John Dick and Graham Stevenson. The site was on a hill, some distance from the nearest railway, so completed locomotives had to be taken through the streets of the town, apparently sometimes under

Electric tram locomotive by Dick, Kerr designed by Frederico Lacroze for the Buenos Aires tramway, from the Electric Railway Journal, 1909.

their own steam, though how this could be achieved with an unsteerable engine is a mystery. They began manufacturing locomotives in 1864, with most of their known output being 0-4-0 saddle tanks, though there is a record of one 0-6-0 tank of unknown date.

They were not the only manufacturers in Airdrie. The Airdrie Iron Company was a general engineering firm who began building locomotives in 1869, and the only engines for which we have definite information were all 0-4-0 saddle tanks. The works closed in 1913.

Gibb & Hogg was another general engineering company, established at Airdrie in 1866, who began manufacturing locomotives in the 1890s, again concentrating on 0-4-0 saddle tanks but also with the occasional 0-6-0ST.

Scott Sinclair of Greenock was primarily a shipbuilding company, but they began building locomotives in 1847, with three 2-2-2s for the Caledonian Railway. After that they built all their engines for the Scottish Central Railway, starting with nine more 2-2-2s and ending with five 0-4-2s in 1849. Scotland had several more companies who produced small numbers of locomotives. These and other similar companies from the rest of Britain will be listed with minimum details at the end of the book.

Wales is, of course, famous as the site of the first definitely recorded running of a steam locomotive on rails. The first Welsh company we shall be looking at, Neath Abbey, could well have made an appearance in Chapter One as one of the pioneers. But as they were isolated and had little impact on the development of locomotives it seemed more appropriate to give them pride of place in this review of Welsh manufacturers. Like the early locomotives of north east England, they began manufacturing engines mainly for tramways. Their first engine of 1829 was for the 4ft 2in gauge Sirhowey tramway, built to serve the local iron works. It was a conventional engine for the time, with vertical cylinders, attached to the midpoint of the boiler, driving through a system of levers to a pair of coupled wheels. Their later engines, however, had several very different features. In 1830, they built an 0-6-0 engine for the 3ft 6in gauge Gloucester & Cheltenham Railway. Two extraordinary engines were built for the Dowlais iron works tramway, which was notable for having several sections that would have been too steep for a conventional locomotive. To overcome that problem, sections of the line were converted to rack and pinion, and the 0-6-0 locomotive was fitted with a cog that could be lowered down to engage with the rack when needed. It was not the first rack and pinion locomotive, but the Middleton Colliery forerunner was only bult to provide extra adhesion for a light locomotive. The Neath Abbey engine could be considered as the first to be built to overcome steep slopes – an idea that would reappear decades later in mountain railways. The other interesting engine was a geared engine with two four-coupled unit, making an 0-4-4-0 arrangement. The inclined cylinders connected with a central jack shaft, with a gear wheel, that connected with gears on the two central axles. Two of these engines were built, one for Dowlais and the other for Rhymney Forge. Neath Abbey continued to make locomotives in small numbers until the 1870s, although later engines were more conventional, including a number of tank engines and standard gauge locomotives for the Monmouthshire Railway and Canal Co.

The next important manufacturer in Wales was De Winton, begun by Owen Thomas in Caernarfon in 1840, who was later joined by Jeffreys Parry De Winton. The company began by supplying cast iron street furniture, later developing an important business in building marine steam engines. They began building locomotives in 1869, concentrating on narrow gauge locomotives for the Welsh slate industry. All the locomotives were 0-4-0s, with vertical boilers. They continued supplying these engines to the industry until at least 1897. During this period they received an order from the Dinorwic quarry at Llanberis, now home to the National Slate Museum. Interestingly, they not only supplied locomotives but also equipped the extensive slate workshops including the imposing 50ft diameter water wheel.

One other early manufacturer deserves a special mention – the Tredegar Iron Works. This takes us right back to the beginnings of railway history, as the works were owned by Samuel Homfray, who had been responsible for inviting Richard Trevithick to build a locomotive for his Penydarren works in 1828. The company had already acquired a locomotive from Robert Stephenson & Co in 1829, and Thomas Ellis, the chief engineer at the works, used this as the basis for building his own 0-6-0 locomotive *St. David* that was set to work on the 4ft 2in gauge line. When this was converted to standard gauge, the engine continued in use on the company's own internal rail network. Ellis was to supervise the building of nine more locomotives but perhaps his greatest contribution to railway development came when he took on an apprentice and trained him. His name was Daniel Gooch.

The only other Welsh manufacturer whose output ran into double figures was Parfitt & Jackson of Cardiff, whose main line was general engineering and shipbuilding, but between 1869 and 1881 built locomotives for the Marquis of Bute Railway, later the Cardiff Railway, that joined the Bute Docks to Pontypridd. They supplied a total of thirteen 0-6-0 saddle tanks between 1869 and 1881.

Few locomotives were built by independent engineering companies in Ireland. The most important was Thomas Grendon & Co, established as a general engineering works at Drogheda in the 1830s, who began building their own locomotives in1845. Over the next three years they built a series of 2-2-2s for the 5ft 3in Dublin & Drogheda and the Midland & Great Western railways, notable for their very tall domes, set just behind the chimney. These two lines remained their most important clients, though over the years, there were small variations with some 0-4-2, 2-4-0 and 0-6-0s and one 2-2-2 tank for the Midland & Great Western. Similar broad gauge engines were built for the Great Southern & Western, Dundalk & Enniskillen and the Newry, Warrenpoint & Rostrevor railways. Their final locomotive was a 2-4-0 standard gauge locomotive for the Belfast & Northern Counties Railway.

The other Irish independent was William Spence of the Cork Street Foundry in Dublin. Their entire output consisted of eighteen locomotives for the 1ft 10in gauge Guinness Brewery line. These were unusual locomotives, though outwardly resembling many other 4-wheeled tram engines, with built up sides, the cylinders and crankshaft were above the boiler, with vertical connecting rods to the rear wheels. They were built between 1887 and 1921.

Chapter Thirteen

An English Miscellany

In this chapter we shall be looking at some of the more important or particularly interesting manufacturers, who have not been covered earlier. They will be treated in chronological order, based on the dates when they began manufacturing locomotives, which brings the general engineering firm Mether Dixon, founded in Liverpool in 1826, to the top of the list. They began in 1827 by building a small tank engine and two locomotive cranes for use at their own works, after which there was a gap of six years before they began manufacturing for other lines. In 1833 they built two 0-4-0 engines for the 5ft gauge Petersburg Railroad, that ran from Petersburg, Virginia to Garysburg, North Carolina, followed by 2-2-0 the following year. They were designed by Edward Bury, who also had works in Liverpool, and had already delivered a first engine to the line but had too much work in hand to complete the rest of the order. Several orders followed for more local concerns, including the Liverpool and Birkenhead Docks and nearby collieries. The only overseas order was three 0-4-0s for Russia. By 1838 they had rationalised their output by building four six-wheeled engines – 0-4-2, 0-6-0, 2-2-2 and 2-4-0 that were intended as display examples to show to potential customers. In 1837, they sold six 2-2-2s to the Liverpool & Manchester, but their most unusual engines were built for the GWR broad gauge in 1837 and 1838. They were 2-2-2 locomotives, distinguished by the unusual solid wheels, and the size of the drive wheels, 7ft and 8ft. Over the next few years, they continued supplying mainly 2-2-2 engines to various lines in Britain and by 1843, they had built a total of seventy-five locomotives, mainly 2-2-2s. The company was dissolved in that year, but the name Mather soon reappeared in a quite different business, manufacturing gunpowder and iron.

As already mentioned, some of the Mather jobs came to them because Edward Bury had too much work in hand. Bury had been in a partner in a steam sawmill in 1823 but left in 1826 to set up on his own as an iron founder and general engineer, later moving to a new site in Liverpool, near the Clarence Docks on the Leeds & Liverpool, hence the name Clarence Foundry. He hired James Kennedy, who had worked with the Stephensons as works foreman. Later he became a partner and the name changed to Edward Bury & Co. He had originally intended to compete in the Rainhill trials with a six-wheeled engine, *Dreadnought,* but was unable to get it ready on time. It was later tried on the Liverpool & Manchester but rejected by George Stephenson and was eventually sold to the Bolton & Leigh Railway. He followed that with an 0-4-0, *Liverpool,* which showed the features that were to typify his locomotives. There was a wrought iron bar frame within the wheels, near-horizontal inside cylinders and a domed firebox.

Bury was unusual among manufacturers in that he also became directly employed by a railway company, the London & Birmingham. At first, he had a decidedly unusual role as Contractor for Locomotive Power, which required him both to supply and maintain locomotives, for which he was paid a farthing a mile for passenger trains and a halfpenny a mile for goods. This, not surprisingly, proved unworkable, and he was appointed instead as a conventional manager of the locomotive department. The company seemed not to be concerned about any clash of interests, with their locomotive manager ordering locomotives form his own manufacturing company – a position the Stephensons had avoided. He continued to favour four-wheeled locomotives, and altogether 110 2-2-0s were built, mainly for British lines. Meanwhile, Bury had been appointed as chief engineer for

Edward Bury locomotive *Liverpool* of 1828, seen here as modified in 1830.

the Birmingham & Gloucester and later to the L&NWR. Eventually, the company began building six-wheeled engines in different configurations for the London & Birmingham. In 1842, there was another name change and the company became Bury, Curtis & Kennedy. Edward Bury himself retired in 1848 but the company continued to operate until 1851.

Rothwell, Hick & Rothwell of Bolton was established around 1830 and when one of the partners, Benjamin Hick, went to the Rainhill trials, he returned enthused with the idea of building locomotives. At this point, Hick decided to begin his own business, which we shall look at shortly, leaving the old company manufacturing under the name, Rothwell & Co. They were quick to recognise that railways would soon be spreading across many different countries, and many would be looking to Britain to supply their locomotives. Their first order was a 2-2-0 for the Bolton & Leigh Railway in 1831, but a year later they sent their second engine across the Atlantic to the Pontchartrain Railroad, linking the Mississippi at New Orleans to the Lake Pontchartrain. The company had ordered an earlier locomotive from another company, which had failed, so the Rothwell was the first locomotive to run a service on the line. Other American orders included a 4-2-0 for the 5ft gauge South Carolina Railroad and there was also an order for a line in Canada. European orders came from the Paris & Versailles and the Leipzig & Dresden railways. At home, their main orders came from the Grand Junction and the London & Birmingham in the 1830s.

An imposing Rothwell locomotive built for the Bristol & Exeter broad gauge.

The 1840s saw a large number of 2-4-0 locomotives being built for the GWR and the home market became increasingly important, with L&SWR being their biggest customer.

Between 1846 and 1848 they supplied twenty-nine 2-2-2 locomotives. So far, the engines had been conventional, but in the 1850s they began supplying locomotives to the Bristol & Exeter Railway. Designed by James Pearson, the engines had a 4-2-4 wheel arrangement, with 9ft diameter flangeless drive wheels. With a domeless boiler and with leading and trailing bogies, these immense engines were unlike anything else the company built. They proved not only to be powerful but also speedy and were recorded at 82mph when descending Wellington Bank. Other large orders came for Alexander Allan designed locomotives for the Lancaster & Carlisle, 2-4-0 goods and 2-2-2 passenger engines. Orders, however, began to dry up in the 1860s, and among their last products was a pair of 4-4-0 saddle tanks for the Carmarthen & Cardigan Railway. The company stopped making locomotives in 1864, and part of the premises were sold off.

Benjamin Hick started his new works, also in Bolton, in 1833 and was joined by his two sons, although one left after a year. When Benjamin died in 1842, John Hick carried on the business and was later joined by William Hargreaves, at which point the company became Hick, Hargreaves & Co. The first locomotive of 1833 was a vertical boiler steam rail carriage for Thomas Lever Rushton, a Bolton banker, who was involved in railway development in the area. It was an unusual vehicle, with three cylinders driving a crankshaft, that engaged with two gears on the driving axle – a simple clutch allowed either gear to be used. This was followed by an engine for the Pontchartrain Railroad – one can assume that Hick had been involved in securing the order for the first engine for the line while still a partner with Rothwell. In a reversal of the trade between Britain and America, John Norris built a 4-2-0 locomotive for the Birmingham & Gloucester Railway based on a design he had demonstrated on the Belmont Incline, which at one point had nearly 200ft at a gradient of I in 15, and which he then developed for the Baltimore & Ohio Railroad.

It was this success that encouraged the British company to order an engine that would be capable of dealing with the notorious Lickey Incline, after Edward Bury had claimed that no locomotive would be powerful enough to climb it. The engine had outside cylinders set by the smoke box, connected to drive wheels in front of the firebox. A unique feature for the time was the four-wheel front swivelling bogie. Hick was to build other locomotives based on the Norris original. After the 1830s, the company's only exports were two 2-2-2s for the Paris & Versailles Railway in 1840.

Hick continued manufacturing locomotives for a number of British railways until 1850, when they delivered the last of eight 2-2-2s to the Birkenhead railway. They had never concentrated on locomotive construction and the company continued as a general engineering firm. The Hargreaves family finally sold their share in 1968, after which the company passed through different owners, and in 2002 finally left their original site for a new location, but still in Bolton.

The Haigh Foundry in Wigan was briefly mentioned in Chapter I and we can now take up the story from the time when they became seriously engaged in locomotive construction in 1835 as the Haigh Foundry Co. under new owners. Like others already mentioned, they began as sub-contractors for Edward Bury, building a number of his standard 0-4-0s. They continued building for other railways, starting with three 2-2-2s for the Liverpool & Manchester in 1836. They then went on mainly building for British lines, though in 1838 they supplied two 2-2-2s to the Paris & St. Germain railway. Most of their output was conventional, but in 1838 they provided two 2-2-2s to the GWR with 6ft 4in drive wheels and gears set at a 3:2 ratio. They were not a success, and the gearing was removed and shortly afterwards largely rebuilt with larger cylinders and new valve gear. They were to build for the broad gauge again between 1851 and 1853, this time to designs supplied by Daniel Gooch. Many of their engines were equipped with their own valve gear, using four eccentrics. They continued construction until 1858, their last locomotive being a Crampton with 6ft 6in drive wheels.

James Nasmyth is a name most closely associated with the design and manufacture of machine tools He had worked with the other great machine tool designer, Henry Maudsley until 1831, when he left to set up on his own at in London, before moving to the Bridgewater Foundry at Patricroft on the Bridgewater Canal near Eccles in 1836. He began locomotive construction in 1839, mostly taking on work from Edward Bury and Geroge Stephenson. Among their early productions were two Firefly Class for the GWR and in the 1840s they constructed six powerful 4-2-0s based on the American Norris locomotives, specifically designed to overcome the Lickey Incline on the Birmingham & Gloucester. There was a pause in 1842, and construction only restarted in 1845. In 1850, the company name was changed to James Nasmyth, the first of several name changes over the next few years, ending as Nasmyth Wilson in 1867. Overseas business became hugely important for the company in later years, with locomotives being shipped to Asia, South America, Africa and New Zealand. The latter received the world's first 2-6-2 Prairie locomotive.

During the First World War they built twenty 2-8-0s for the Chemin de fer de l'État. In 1938 they completed their last order for two 2-6-4Ts for South Indian Railways, but the company itself continued in operation. One of its main products was that essential tool of the railway manufacturing workshop, the steam hammer, which James Nasmyth himself had designed in 1839 and which had been a mainstay of the company ever since. It was taken over for war work in 1939 but the Nasmyth firm was never revived. Over the century they had been in existence, they had built 1,307 locomotives.

Thomas Richardson & Sons was based on the Castle Eden Foundry in Hartlepool and they began locomotive construction in 1840 with four 0-6-0 locomotives for the Hartlepool Railway. Their locomotives were all supplied to railways in the north of England and in the 1840s they took over building many engines for Robert Stephenson & Co. Their most important client was the York, Newcastle & Berwick Railway, again 0-6-0s. The company stopped manufacturing locomotives in 1857 and concentrated on marine engines.

Tulk & Ley began business in Whitehaven in 1793 as hardware manufacturers and began manufacturing locomotives in 1840 with two 2-2-2s for the Maryport & Carlisle Railway. They built six 4-2-0 and four 2-2-2 Cramptons, the first two of which were originally intended for Namur in Belgium, hence their names *Namur* and *Liege*, but construction of the line was delayed and they were bought instead by the South Eastern Railway. They were both notable for their 7ft drive wheels. In 1857, the company was taken over by Fletcher Jennings, who decided to concentrate entirely on tank engines. In 1884, the company became Lowca engineering and continued in business until 1912, when fire destroyed most of the factory. Altogether, 245 locomotives were constructed at the works.

The name Thomas Brassey is famous in railway history as a contractor. With his company Brassey, Jackson Betts & Co. he was responsible for constructing railways around the world. It is not, however, a name immediately associated with locomotive construction. One of his most important contracts was for the Grand Trunk Railroad in Canada, for which he was not only to supply all the necessary materials, including the iron work for the immense tubular bridge across the St. Lawrence, but also locomotives. To do so required a new factory being built at Birkenhead, which was named the Canada Works. They began sending out a number of 2-2-2 and 2-4-0 locomotives to Canada in 1854. Brassey's worldwide work as a contractor ensured a regular supply of orders from around the world, with locomotives going to lines in Europe, South America, India and Australia. One of their more interesting locomotives was built for the Mount Cenis Railway across the Alps, linking France and Italy. To overcome the gradients, the Fell system was used. The works remained open until 1880, but locomotive construction appears to have stopped by 1875.

James Cross was locomotive engineer for the St. Helens & Runcorn Gap Railway but when that company was taken over by the L&NWR in 1864, the old workshops at the Sutton Engineering Works in St. Helens were no longer needed, and he took them over. He specialised in tank engines at first and the company would be unremarkable if it had not built the very first Fairlie double-ended locomotives. The first *Progress* was constructed for the Neath & Brecon Railway in 1865. It was not entirely successful, although it already had a typical Fairlie arrangement of two connected four-wheel bogies and a central cab. There was, however, a problem with the steam pipes, which had to be flexible to allow for the movement of the two bogies and they were prone to fracture. There was also a problem with the firebox that served both boilers. A second engine of a similar type, but with modifications, was built for the Anglesey Central Railway. Neither proved reliable, having the sort of teething problems so often connected with novel prototypes, but they led the way to more successful developments. From 1866-8, the whole output consisted of 2-4-0 locomotives for the 5ft 6in gauge East Indian Railway. After that the works closed.

Gilkes Wilson & Co of Middlesborough began in business repairing locomotives in 1843 and commenced building a series of 2-4-0 and 0-6-0 locomotives for a variety of British companies as well as tank engines for local collieries. They have earned, if that is the word, a place in railway history for their role in helping to construct the Tay railway bridge that collapsed in 1879. The ironwork for which they were responsible came in for particular criticism.

J. Scarisbrick Walker established an iron works in Wigan in 1864 and began manufacturing locomotives in 1872. In 1874 he was joined by his brothers and moved to the Pagefield Ironworks, also in Wigan. They specialised at first in building tank engines, mainly supplying collieries. By 1888 they had abandoned steam locomotive construction. In 1907, they turned to building road vehicles, staring with a petrol engine truck and then, in 1932 they returned to railway construction with a series of diesel railcars. They were supplied to many different railways, but by far the most important client was Victorian Railways in Australia. They needed to modernise their fleet after the Second World War and placed their first order in 1948 of twelve 102hp railcars, six 153hp railcars with trailers and ten 153hp railcars. They were eventually to provide sixty-four units, which were given a handsome blue and gold livery. Locomotive production ceased in 1953.

William Wilkinson designed a steam tram engine at his foundry in Wigan in the 1880s. It had a vertical boiler and drive was transmitted through gearing on the crankshaft to the coupled wheels. He improved the design of his engine by adding a condenser on the roof in 1886. Although he was only able to build a few of the locomotives himself, several locomotives of this design were built by other companies, notably Beyer Peacock.

Two companies were established in Bristol, Stother, Slaughter & Company and Fox Walker. The former was the first to start work in 1841 and began by constructing broad gauge locomotives for the GWR and then the Bristol and Exter Railways. In 1844, the name was changed to Avonside after their riverside site at Hotwells. Later they acquired the adjoining shipyard and Henry Stothart took charge of the shipbuilding side of the business. Throughout the 1850s, they built large numbers of locomotives for overseas customers in Europe, South America, India, New Zealand and Australia. They did not neglect the home market, and one of their outstanding locomotives was the first ever 0-8-0 tank engines for the Vale of Neath Railway. In later years, they built large numbers of both Fairlie and Fell locomotives, but in the early 1880s Edward Slaughter died, and the company ran into financial difficulties and Edwin Walker came across from Fox Walker to take over, though keeping the old name. They decided to concentrate entirely on industrial locomotives, mainly tank engines. An outstanding exception was the set of three 2-6-4T engines, built as three-cylinder compounds. In 1905, the company moved to new premises at Fishponds to the east of the city centre, where the extra space available meant they were able to take orders for more large locomotives. The twentieth century, however, was not kind to the company, which, like many others, suffered in the general trade recession. In 1934, they went into voluntary liquidation.

Fox Walker began manufacturing locomotives at the Atlas Works in the St. George district of Bristol in 1864 and specialised, like Avonside, in industrial locomotives, mainly tank engines. They did, however, also begin building steam

Avoncroft Locomotive No.1 supplied to the North Mount Lyell Railway, Tasmania in 1900.

trams, beginning in 187 with a vehicle for the Bristol Tramway, that had opened two years earlier, using horses. They also supplied larger engines, such as the 4-4-0 tender engine built for the Windsor & Annapolis Railroad in Canada in 1868. In 1880, the business was taken over by Peckett & Sons and continued to specialise in saddle tank engines, available in four or six-coupled versions. There were the occasional exceptions, including a 4-4-0T for the 3ft gauge Schill & Skibbereen Tramway in Ireland. Pecketts were famous for reliability, which explains why over seventy of their locomotives are preserved on railways in Britain and abroad. They continued making steam locomotives up to 1958 and attempted to keep the business profitable by moving into the diesel locomotive market, This proved unsuccessful, and they were bought out in 1968, but the new company only survived for three more years before going into liquidation.

The Metropolitan Railway Carriage and Wagon Company, formed in 1863, was, as the name suggests, primarily involved in manufacturing rolling stock. In 1902, it merged with other companies to form Metropolitan Amalgamated, and it was now that they took an important role in railway history. In association with Briths Westinghouse, they started building electric locomotives for use on the Metropolitan Railway with Westinghouse electric gear in 1906. The first batch were known as 'camel backs' because of their raised central can. They were used with conventional rolling stock on the company's suburban routes. There were to be more mergers over the next few years, amalgamating Westinghouse, Metropolitan and Vickers to form Metropolitan-Vickers. They began building new electric locomotives for the line with a more conventional cab in the front of the locomotive in 1923, and the engines remained in use until the line was electrified to Amersham in 1961. One of the locomotives, No.5, *Sarah Siddons*, has been preserved and was run over the route in 2019 to mark the 150th anniversary of the opening of the District Line. In 1929, there was another change when the railway business was taken over by the ship building company Cammell Laird to form Metro-Cammell. The company then began building locomotives for the whole London underground system, from the 1930s right up to the late 1980s, and also supplied stock for other underground railways, including lines in Glasgow and Hong Kong. In 1989, the company was sold to GEC Alsthom, who continued supplying the London Underground and in 2005, they built their last, the Pendelino tilting train.

Davey, Paxman was a well established engineering company, manufacturing a variety of steam engines from stationary engines to traction engines. Ther first locomotive, about which little is known, was built for an 18in gauge line in South Africa. The next is very well known. The Ravenglass & Eskdale Railway was opened in 1875 as a 30in line, designed

Romney, Hythe & Dymchurch Railway 4-6-2 No.2 Northern Chief built by Davey Paxman, 1925.

to bring material down from the Lakeland quarries to the coast. It closed in 1915. This might have been the end, but the famous model railway builder Bassett-Lowke had been looking for an opportunity to run trains on a long 15in gauge track, and he took over the line. It needed a heavy duty locomotive, which would be able to continue the freight business, but at the same time head busy passenger trains in the holiday season. The locomotive *River Esk* was supplied by Paxman in 1922, the first 2-8-2 locomotive to be built in Britain. Following that, another 15in gauge line was being planned by two wealthy enthusiasts, the Romney, Hythe and Dymchurch and again Davey, Paxman built the locomotives, five 4-6-2s and two 4-8-2s, in 1925-6. All eight of these engines have not only survived but remain in use. No more steam locomotives were built, but the company continued in railway construction, supplying a variety of diesel and diesel-electric engines, most famously for the HST (Intercity 125) introduced by British Rail in 1972, constructed at Crewe.

This miscellany ends with one of the most important suppliers of industrial locomotives for both standard and narrow gauge lines, Kerr Stuart. The company was founded in Glasgow by James Kerr in 1881 as dealers in all kinds of railway equipment, including locomotives. When new locomotives were required, they were supplied from a number of sources, including the California Works at Stoke-on-Trent. In 1893, the works were taken over by James Kerr and they began building locomotives under a new name, James Kerr & Co, shortly to become Kerr Stuart. They built a large number of conventional side and saddle tank engines, and later added tender engines, but their main output consisted of narrow gauge engines. Among the former were 12 unusual 0-4-0Ts for the São Paulo Railway, a 5ft 3in gauge that included a number of inclines all worked by cable and stationary engines to cross the Sierras. With increased traffic on the line, it was decided to introduce an extra line, the Serra Nova, running for three miles alongside one of the 8% gradient existing inclines. Again, there were stationary steam engines for cable haulage, but the Kerr Stuart engines were also used, but fitted with a spec1al system that could grip the steel cable when necessary, hence the name "locobreque" – brake engine. In the 1920s they built a number of standard gauge tender locomotives, including fifty standard Class 4 0-6-0s for the LMS.

Their narrow gauge engines were supplied to countries throughout the world. They were mainly tank engines, though they would also take on more exotic orders that included an articulated Meyer 0-6-6-0 for a mining company in Chile. Among their most successful classes was the aptly named, diminutive Wrens. The prototype was an 0-4-0 saddle tank built in 1903 for the Southend Gas Company's 2ft 1¾in gauge line. The following year this was adapted for a 75 cm gauge line near Bilbao, a notable feature of which were the wheels at just 1ft 8in diameter. Over the years, there were to be many changes to the basic design, including adapting some for oil burning, by adding saddle tanks to carry the fuel. Altogether 163 of these sturdy little machines were completed. The company also produced a number of engine units for rail motors.

Kerr Stuart suffered like so many others in the 1920s and although they experimented successfully in trying to adapt to the new demand for diesel locomotives, the works closed in 1930, when goodwill was taken over by Hunslet. It has been estimated that during their time in operation, the works turned out around 1500 locomotives.

Chapter Fourteen

Minor Players

There were a large number of companies which, though they might be important in other fields, made just a few locomotives. To round up this review of British independents, they will be listed in alphabetical order, with brief notes on their output:

Daniel Adamson & Co. of Manchester built nine standard gauge tank engines and four narrow gauge tank engines, 1866-96.

Airdrie Iron Co. may have built up to thirty locomotives between 1869 and 1913.

Atkinson-Walker Waggons Ltd., Preston, built locomotives 1926-31, with vertical boilers.

Balmforth Bros., PAEL Inge Foundry, Rodley, built at least three vertical boiler locomotives. C.1876.

Barr & McNabb, Paisley, built three locomotives for Scottish railways in 1840.

Bedford Engineering Co., Bedford, built a few, exact number unknown, vertical boiler locomotives.

Bellis & Seekings, Birmingham, built two well tank engines for Pyke Bros china clay industry narrow gauge line, 1866, 1872.

Blaenavon Co. iron works are known to have built three saddle tanks. The remains of the foundry are now listed as a UNESCO World Heritage site.

J.G. Bodmer, Manchester, built a number of locomotives and designed others, built by Sharp Roberts. The first locomotive, 1834 was an unusual 2-2-0 with two pistons per cylinder, one set driving conventionally, the other through crossheads and linkages, set at 180° to the cranks on the wheels.

Bolckow Vaughan & Co. Ltd., Middlesborough, were mainly concerned with rebuilding old locomotives but also built a few locomotives before being taken over by Dorman Long in 1929.

Peter Borrie & Co., Dundee, built five locomotives in 1841but apparently only sold one of them. The following year they were bankrupt.

E. Borrows & Sons, St. Helens, built a total of forty engines for local industries, all 0-4-0 well tanks.

I.W. Boulton, Ashton-Under-Lyne, built a number of locomotives, many made up from parts scavenged from other engines, 1856-76. Original engines were geared.

R. Brotherhood, Chippenham, built mainly tank engines, 1857-67, including two broad gauge 0-6-0Ts but also two 0-6-0s.

Brown & May, Devizes, built two vertical boiler, geared locomotives.

Caird & Co., Greenock, built four 2-2-2s for Scottish railways in 1840.

Christie, Adams & Hill, Rotherhithe, built six 2-2-2 for the L&SWR, 1848-9.

John Coulthard & Son, Gateshead, began constructing in 1835 and had built some twenty locomotives by 1865 when the works were taken over by Black Hawthorn.

Davies & Metcalfe, Manchester, built two 2-6-0T engines for the narrow gauge Vale of Rheidol Railway in 1902

D. Drummond & Son, Govan: the company was founded by the very successful engineer, Dugald Drummond in 1891, but enjoyed only modest success, with a small number of narrow gauge engines being built and two railmotors. In 1895, he left the company to take a post as engineer for the London & South Western Railway, leaving his sons to run it as Glasgow Railway Engineering

Thomas Edington, Glasgow, built four 2-2-2s in 1840-1 Co. Ltd.

Fawcett Preston & Co., Liverpool, built just one 0-6-0 in 1848.

Fodens, Sandbach, built just one locomotive in 1930.

Geo. Forrester & Co., Liverpool, built locomotives between 1834 and 1847, mainly outside cylinder 2-2-2s but they received an order for fifteen 2-4-0s that year for the South Eastern Railway.

Fossick & Hackworth, Stockton-on-Tees, was established by George Fossick and John Hackworth, Timothy's brother, in 1834. It is perhaps a little unfair to call them minor players as they produced over 100 locomotives, but with little variation, almost all 6-wheeled tender engines apart from four tank locomotives.

Galloway, Bowman & Glasgow, Manchester, built one and possibly two locomotives – the second might have been a rebuild of the first – in1831.

Gibb & Hogg, Airdrie, built twenty saddle tank engines, 1898-1905.

John Harris, Darlington, built twelve locomotives, of which three are known to have been 0-4-0 saddle tanks, 1863-9.

Hartley Arnoux & Fanning, Stoke-on-Trent, mostly produced twenty-one locomotives for Kerr Stuart to their design, who later took over the company.

Hawks & Thomson, Gateshead, built three locomotives for the Newcastle & Carlisle, 1837-8.

J. & E. Headly, Cambridge, only built one vehicle, but it was very strange, in effect, an early form of railmotor, with a four-wheeled locomotive section to which was attached a small inspection car.

Head Wrightson, Stockton-on-Tees, built several 0-4-0T engines, but were chiefly known for vertical boilered geared locomotives in the 1860s and 1870s.

John Hopper, Fencehouses, built one 0-6-0T in 1870.

A. Horlock & Co., Northfleet, built two unusual locomotives for the 4ft gauge Dinorwic quarry. The 0-4-0 engines had inclined cylinders near the smokebox, with connecting rods to the large rear wheels set at the firebox.

Ince Forge, Wigan, built one 2-4-0 saddle tank for the broad gauge South Devon Railway in 1871

Johnston & McNab, Port Dundas, built a 0-4-0 for the Garnick & Glasgow Railway in 1832.

J & G. Joicey, Newcastle, were a company primarily involved in providing machinery for collieries, including winding engines, but built locomotives between 1867 and 1894. One known locomotive was a narrow gauge 0-4-0 side tank for the Gateshead Gas company.

Kirtley & Co., Warrington, built locomotives from 1837-41 including five 2-2-2s for the Leipzig & Dresden Railway.

Kitching & Co, Darlington, built for the S&DR from1835-60, apart from one for the Clarnece Railway and two for the Whitehaven & Furness.

Stephen Lewin, Poole, built narrow gauge locomotives and a tram engine for Bilbao, 1868-79

Lingford Gardiner Co. Ltd. Bishop Auckland, built an undetermined number of tank engines 1900-31, those known were all 0-4-0ST.

Linton, Selby, built two locomotives for the York & North Midland, 1842

William Lister, Darlington, bult six locomotives 1838-40 based on Timothy Hackworth designs.

Longbotham, Barnsley, built one 0-6-0T c.1847.

Manlove Alliot & Fryer, Nottingham, designed a double-decker steam rail car in 1876. It is not known how many were built.

William Marshall, Gravesend, appear to have built at least one locomotive for the London & Greenwich Railway c.1834

John Melling, Rainhill, built three locomotives for the Grand Junction Railway, 1841-2.

Neasham & Welch built one locomotive for the S&DR, 1840.

Nicholls, Williams & Co, Tavistock, built one locomotive for Devon Great Consols copper mine, 1850.

Oliver & Co. Ltd., Chesterfield, began constructing 0-4-0 saddle tanks in 1888 and continued to do so after being taken over by Markham & Co. Ltd in 1899. There was also one 0-6-0ST built in 1909. The last was built 1914.

Parfitt & Jenkins, Cardiff, built 13 0-6-0STs for the Marquis of Bute's Railway, 1869-81.

Pearson & Knowles Coal & iron Co. Ltd., Warrington, began constructing locomotives for their own use in 1899 but later built for other companies, mostly 0-4-0ST and 0-6-0STs.

Peel, William & Peel, Ancoats, were a major engineering company but only built two locomotives, both in 1839.

Ransomes & Rapier, Ipswich, are notable for their part in supplying material and locomotives for the 2ft 6in gauge Woosung Railway, the first in China that opened in 1876. They later built narrow gauge diesels.

Riley Brothers, Stockton-on-Tees, are said to have built one vertical boilered 0-4-0T in 1890. On a personal note, I was delighted to find this one as one of the three founding Riley brothers was my great grandfather.

Roberston & Henderson, Glasgow, built a vertical boiler railcar, 1877.

Robinson, Thomas & Sons Ltd, Rochdale, built a few locomotives, the actual number uncertain but included a vertical boiler engine for their own use and a tender locomotive for New Zealand.

Sandys, Carne & Vivian, Hayle, are said to have built the first railway locomotive in Cornwall for the Hayle Railway, opened in 1837.

Sara & Co., Plymouth, built one geared locomotive with a vertical boiler for the South Devon Railway in 1888.

Sara & Burgess, Falmouth, built four broad gauge vertical boiler locomotives in the 1860s.

Savile Street Foundry, Sheffield, built a tram engine in 1882 and a steam railcar.

Alexander Shanks & Son, Arbroath, built a dozen 0-4-0 saddle tanks, 1972-7.

Silley Cox & Co. Ltd., Falmouth, built a similar engine to the Sara & Cox in 1918.

John Smith, Coven, built perhaps as many as twenty 0-4-0 and 0-6-0 tank engines, 1863-74.

Thomas Spittle, Newport, Monmouth, was a well-established ironworks that built six 0-4-2Ts, 1877-99.

Stark & Fulton, Glasgow, built nine 2-2-0 and one 2-2-2, 1839-49.

Summers, Groves & Day, Southampton, built a 2-2-2 for the Richmond, Fredericksburg & Potomac Railroad in 1837 and are known to have built some locomotives for the London & Southampton Railway.

H.E. Taylor, Chester, built five 3ft 6in gauge locomotives for the John Bazley White cement works, 1877-85.

J & A Taylor, Ayre, built just one 0-4-0ST, c. 1870.

Thornwell & Warham, Burton-on-Trent, built locomotives for the local breweries, 1840-90.

Thwaites & Carbutt, Bradford, built one very unusual locomotive in 1848 in which the single cylinder was placed between the drive wheels at right angles to the boiler. They also built three conventional 0-6-0s.

Leonard J. Todd, Leith, built one locomotive for the Tranvias de Santander, a tramway system opened in 1875.

Richard Walker & Brother, Bury, were unusual in that although the company built twenty locomotives between 1847 and 1854, they were all for East Lancashire Railway of which Richard Walker was a director.

The Worcester Engine Company had a brief career, manufacturing locomotives building mainly 0-6-0 goods from 1865-70, but in that time they built seventy engines.

Select Bibliography

Baker, A.C. and Civil, T.D. Allen, *Bagnall Locomotives,* 1990

Bailey, Michael R., *Loco Motion, The World's Oldest Steam Locomotives,* 2014

Binns, D., *Articulated Locomotives of the World,* 1975

Burton, Anthony, *The Locomotive Pioneers,* 2017

Burton, Anthony and Scott Morgan, John, *Victorian and Edwardian Locomotives* (2 volumes), 2024

Clark, E.R., *Kitsons of Leeds,* 1938

Dempsey, G.D. and Kinnear Clark, D., *Victorian Steam Locomotives,* 2022

Larkin, Edgar R. and John G., *The Railway Workshops of Britain,* 1988

Lowe, James W., *British Steam Locomotive Builders,*2014

Reed, Brian, *150 Years of British Steam Locomotives,* 1975

Rolt, L.T.C., *A Hunslet Hundred,* 1964

Smithers, Mark, *Locomotive Builders of Leeds,*2018

Snell, J.B., *Mechanical Engineering: railways,* 1971

Warren, J.G.H., *A Century of Locomotive Building by Robert Stephenson & Co.,* 1923

Young, Robert, *Timothy Hackworth and the Locomotive,* 1923, reprinted 1975